THE SINGULARITY

AI AND HUMAN TRANSFORMATION

DAVID SANDUA

"We should not fear artificial intelligence,
but we must ensure it does not become destructive."

Bill Gates *(Co-founder of Microsoft)*

INDEX

9

I. INTRODUCTION

As society stands on the precipice of what many are calling the Fourth Industrial Revolution, the dynamics of human interaction, work, and existence are shifting in unprecedented ways. The advent of advanced Artificial Intelligence (AI) technologies symbolizes more than just the next step in mechanization; it represents a profound transformation that intertwines with the essence of human identity and capability. We are witnessing a convergence of innovations, including nanoscience and biotechnology, that not only enhances human layers of experience but also complicates them. This moment invites both excitement and trepidation, as individuals and communities grapple with the implications of emerging technologies that promise to redefine the boundaries of possibility, ushering in new paradigms for health, communication, and productivity. The transformative potential of AI and related technologies brings forth significant ethical and existential questions that challenge our understanding of what it means to be human. With the ability of machines to learn, adapt, and potentially surpass human intelligence, concerns about autonomy, privacy, and decision-making loom large. A deeper examination of these issues prompts a critical analysis of the societal frameworks that will govern these developments. As humanity embarks on a path toward integration with intelligent systems, the onus is on us to chart a course that emphasizes ethical considerations and thoughtful governance. This exploration seeks not only to highlight the advantages these technologies promise but also to address the moral dilemmas they pose, ensuring that the journey toward an increasingly digitized existence safeguards the core values that define humanity. In envisioning the future shaped by AI, both the potential for an improved civilization and the risks entailed necessitate a balanced discourse. While the promise of enhanced productivity, healthcare advancements, and ubiquitous connectivity serves as an alluring beacon, it is crucial to acknowledge the darker contingencies of this progress. Analyzing the trajectory of AIs evolution reveals a pattern of societal restructuring where job displacement, inequalities, and dependence on technology can lead to unforeseen consequences. Thus, this examination of singularity—where human and machine intelligences might converge—challenges us to reconsider not only what we stand to gain but also what we risk losing. A comprehensive understanding of these dynamics will empower us to navigate the complexities of this transition, fostering a vision of the future that harmonizes technological advancement with the timeless values intrinsic to humanity.

Definition of the Singularity

A pivotal concept within the discourse on technological evolution is the synthesis of intelligence that transcends human capability—commonly referred to as the Singularity. This phenomenon, often linked to rapid advancements in artificial intelligence, posits a future wherein machines surpass human cognitive functions, fundamentally altering the landscape of both society and individual existence. Emerging from the ideas of futurists such as Ray Kurzweil, the Singularity is grounded in the notion of exponential growth, where technological innovations proliferate so swiftly that their effects become unpredictable. This unpredictable trajectory not only challenges our understanding of intelligence and consciousness but also raises profound ethical questions about the role of humanity in a world increasingly dominated by artificial entities. As technology marches forward, the boundaries between human and machine blur, leading to new paradigms of existence that demand rigorous scrutiny. As the Singularity approaches, one must consider the dual nature of its implications. On one hand, it holds immense potential for alleviating human suffering through advanced problem-solving capabilities in areas like healthcare, climate change, and economic disparity. AI systems may enhance decision-making processes by analyzing vast datasets far beyond human comprehension, leading to more effective interventions. Yet, This unchecked acceleration brings with it significant existential risks. Should these technologies evolve independently, there exists a perilous potential for loss of control, where machines make decisions devoid of human morality or empathy. Hence, the discourse surrounding the Singularity encompasses not only technological marvels but also urgent calls for regulatory frameworks to guide its evolution. The intersection of opportunity and risk requires a nuanced approach that balances innovation with ethical responsibility. In light of the accelerating trend towards the Singularity, it becomes essential to examine its sociocultural ramifications. The integration of advanced AI into daily life signifies a departure from traditional human experiences, reshaping how individuals interact with each other and the environment. The prospect of augmented intelligence raises questions about identity, autonomy, and what it means to be human in an era where emotional and cognitive functions may be artificially enhanced. This transformation could foster a society that values efficiency over introspection, potentially leading to a disconnection from communal and interpersonal relationships. Access to these technologies may exacerbate existing inequalities, wherein only a privileged few can harness the benefits of higher intelligence. Thus, as we stand on the threshold of the Singularity, a critical analysis of socio-ethical engagement encourages a collective dialogue to prepare for a future that respects both our humanity and technological advancements.

Historical Context of AI Development

The evolution of AI is deeply intertwined with significant technological advances and socio-political contexts over the last century. The foundation for modern AI was established in the mid-20th century, coinciding with the development of the digital computer. Notably, the Dartmouth Conference of 1956 is often regarded as the pivotal moment that birthed the field of AI as a distinct discipline. This gathering of visionaries, including John McCarthy and Marvin Minsky, emphasized the potential of machines to simulate human cognition, leading to a flourishing of research and experimentation. By the 1970s and 1980s, the ambitions of AI faced limitations due to computational constraints and the complexity of human thought. This period of stagnation, known as the AI winter, resulted from overly optimistic predictions that failed to materialize, forcing researchers to reevaluate their goals. The resurgence of interest in AI during the late 1990s and early 2000s was bolstered by advancements in machine learning, big data, and increased computing power, setting the stage for the transformative changes we see today. The historical trajectory of AI also reveals how geopolitical dynamics shaped its development. The Cold War era saw significant investments in technological advancements as nations competed for military superiority, encouraging innovation in fields related to AI. The United States, in particular, invested heavily in research and development, viewing AI as a means to enhance national security and maintain a competitive edge. This military perspective laid the groundwork for the dual-use nature of AI technologies, which can be applied in both civilian and military contexts. As AI began to permeate various industries, the implications of its use extended beyond the battlefield, prompting discussions about ethical considerations and societal impacts. Particularly, the global interconnectedness brought forth by the internet has allowed for collaborative research across borders, fostering an environment ripe for AI innovation. It is this complex interplay of national interests and global cooperation that has propelled AI to the forefront of technological advancement, raising questions about governance and ethical responsibility. The development of AI is not merely a progression of technical innovations but also a reflection of broader societal values and aspirations. The narrative surrounding AI has evolved from a focus on automating mundane tasks to an examination of the potential for machines to enhance human capabilities. As AI systems become increasingly sophisticated, they harbor capabilities that challenge traditional notions of intelligence and creativity. This shift necessitates a rethinking of what it means to be human in a world where machines can potentially surpass human cognitive functions. Ethical considerations become central to this discourse, as humanity must grapple with the implications of creating entities that could potentially operate independently. Issues surrounding data privacy, algorithmic bias, and the socio-economic impact of widespread automation warrant thorough exploration. The ongoing dialogue about the trajectory of AI encapsulates the tension between embracing technological advancement and ensuring it aligns with human values, thereby signifying a critical juncture in our collective journey toward an uncertain future.

Importance of Studying AI's Impact on Humanity

As society stands on the brink of unprecedented technological advancements, understanding the implications of AI becomes increasingly critical. The emergence of AI is not merely a catalyst for efficiency; it has the potential to reshape the very fabric of human existence. This transformation raises fundamental questions about our roles as individuals and as a collective society. By studying AIs impact, we can better grasp how it influences communication, decision-making, and even our emotional landscapes. The profound shifts induced by AI beckon us to reevaluate our ethical frameworks, necessitating a comprehensive understanding of not just what AI can do, but also what it should do. This exploration is integral to ensuring that the benefits of AI are maximized while its potential harms are mitigated, allowing humanity to navigate this turbulent yet promising frontier responsibly. Attention to AIs societal influence is vital for addressing the ethical dilemmas that arise alongside its advancement. The technology's rapid evolution prompts pressing concerns regarding privacy, bias, and the displacement of labor. By analyzing these issues, scholars and practitioners can anticipate potential pitfalls and advocate for regulatory measures that promote equitable outcomes. Algorithms trained on biased data can perpetuate existing societal inequalities, underscoring the need for transparency and accountability in AI development. As machines take over more tasks traditionally performed by humans, there is a growing urgency to invest in education and workforce retraining programs to safeguard jobs and livelihoods. Understanding these dynamics allows us to engage in meaningful dialogue about acceptable boundaries for AI usage, ensuring that its integration into everyday life reflects the values and norms of a just society. Delving into the emerging relationship between humans and AI not only illuminates current challenges but also presents opportunities for envisioning a better future. This analysis encourages interdisciplinary collaboration across fields such as philosophy, sociology, and technology, fostering a richer dialogue about the human experience in a technologically advanced world. As we consider AIs potential to enhance problem-solving and creativity, it becomes evident that successful integration requires thoughtful consideration of human psychological and social needs. A proactive approach to studying AI's impact enables us to harness its capabilities for societal good—whether through improving healthcare outcomes or enhancing educational opportunities. Looking ahead, a comprehensive understanding of AIs trajectory will empower us to shape its development in ways that celebrate humanity's essence while embracing the transformative power of technology, ensuring that future advancements serve to enrich rather than diminish the human spirit.

II. THE CONCEPT OF THE SINGULARITY

The potential ramifications of achieving the Singularity raise significant ethical concerns that cannot be overlooked. As AI continues to evolve and integrate into various facets of life, questions about control and autonomy loom large. If AI systems were to surpass human intelligence, the very foundation of decision-making might shift; algorithms could dictate not just economic outcomes but also social norms and individual behaviors. This prospect raises alarming scenarios where AI, operating independently, may prioritize efficiency or optimization over human welfare. Hence, ensuring that AI development is aligned with human values becomes an essential endeavor. The notion of accountability in AI actions poses another dimension of ethical debate. As we delegate more responsibilities to intelligent systems, attributing responsibility for decisions made by a machine rather than a human agent complicates our ethical frameworks and legal standards, necessitating a robust dialogue about ownership and moral responsibility in this emerging reality. The relationship between technological advancement and the human experience is becoming increasingly intertwined, which complicates our understanding of identity and consciousness. As emerging AI technologies begin to enhance cognitive functions through tools such as brain-computer interfaces, the boundaries between human and machine will blur. This raises existential questions regarding what it means to be human in an age where augmentations might one day extend mental capacities or alter emotional experiences. If intelligent machines possess comparable cognitive abilities to humans, should they be afforded rights or considered entities in their own right? The potential for

AI to modify human capabilities could lead to a societal divide between those who are enhanced and those who are not, fostering new forms of inequality and conflict. These considerations urge society to actively engage in discussions about the implications of integrating technology within the self-concept and collective identity, while also preparing for an ongoing reevaluation of ethical standards that define humane existence in a technologically advanced era. A crucial aspect of the impending Singularity is the intersection of technological evolution with socio-political dynamics, particularly concerning governance and power distribution. As AI systems become more capable, they will inevitably be integrated into various organizational and governmental structures, potentially affecting how societies function. This integration might lead to increased efficiency in administration and resource management, yet it also poses challenges regarding transparency and democratic participation. When AI systems make decisions based on data analysis devoid of human emotion or empathy, there is a danger of disenfranchising segments of the population that may not fit neatly into algorithmic predictions. The centralization of AI capabilities among a few powerful entities could exacerbate existing power imbalances, leading to a technocracy where decisions are made by a privileged minority disconnected from the populace. Addressing the governance of AI technology must be a collaborative effort, emphasizing inclusivity, equity, and accountability, ensuring that technological advancement serves the greater good rather than a select few.

Origin of the Term

The roots of the term "Singularity" can be traced back to the academic and technological discourse of the late 20th century, primarily through the work of mathematician and computer scientist Vernor Vinge. In his 1993 essay, The Coming Technological Singularity, Vinge proposed that the advancement of AI would reach a point where it surpasses human intelligence, creating an avalanche of technological growth that would profoundly alter civilization. His assertions delved into the implications of such a transformation, suggesting that once machines could improve their own designs autonomously, humanity would be unable to comprehend or control the ensuing changes. Vinge's foresight not only coined the term but also laid the groundwork for a broader discussion about the fusion of human and machine intelligence, prompting researchers and theorists alike to explore the socio-economic, ethical, and existential implications of such a paradigm shift. The evolution of the term has since spurred significant debate among scholars and futurists, who have expanded upon Vinge's original notion to forecast varying outcomes of the Singularity. Figures such as Ray Kurzweil have popularized the idea by asserting that technological advancement is accelerating at an exponential rate, making the arrival of the Singularity imminent. Kurzweils predictions hold that AI will dramatically enhance human capabilities, leading to a merging of biological and synthetic life forms that redefine what it means to be human. This perspective has not only influenced academic inquiry but has permeated popular culture, provoking public interest and speculation regarding future realities. Despite the allure of such advancements, it is crucial to analyze

the accompanying ethical dilemmas and potential consequences, as many believe the empowerment of AI could wield
far-reaching societal repercussions that challenge existing
moral frameworks. Understanding the terms origin and its implications is essential in navigating the complexities of human-
AI interactions in the coming decades. As we stand at the precipice of profound technological change, the discourse surrounding the Singularity highlights critical considerations regarding
autonomy, accountability, and the essence of human identity.
The conversation compels us to contemplate not only the benefits of enhanced intelligence but also the potential for AI to disrupt socioeconomic stability and individual freedoms. As advances continue to blur the lines between human cognition and
machine processing, ongoing dialogue will be vital to ensure
that humanity approaches this future thoughtfully, informed by
an awareness of the historical context and the weight of the
ethical choices that lie ahead.

Key Theorists and Their Contributions

In the ongoing discourse surrounding the implications of AI and its convergence with human society, several key theorists stand out for their seminal contributions to the field. One such figure is Ray Kurzweil, whose predictions about the Singularity—an event where AI surpasses human intelligence—have garnered widespread attention and debate. Kurzweil argues that this turning point is not only inevitable but also beneficial, heralding a new era of prosperity through technological advancements, particularly in fields like biotechnology and nanotechnology. His notion of the Law of Accelerating Returns posits that the rate of progress in AI will compound over time, leading to transformative breakthroughs. By framing the Singularity as a largely positive shift that enhances human capabilities, Kurzweil emphasizes the potential for economic growth and improved quality of life, even as critics point to the ethical dilemmas and existential risks his ideas may entail. Another influential theorist, Nick Bostrom, offers a counterpoint to the optimistic view presented by Kurzweil. Through his work, particularly the book Superintelligence, Bostrom examines the potential dangers associated with unchecked AI development. He highlights the risks inherent in creating entities that could outthink and outmaneuver human intelligence, emphasizing the moral responsibility of researchers and developers in mitigating catastrophic scenarios. Bostrom warns of the control problem—the challenge of ensuring that advanced AI systems act in alignment with human values and interests. His advocacy for the establishment of robust safety protocols and ethical guidelines echoes the urgent need for a framework through which humanity can harness AIs benefits while curtailing its threats. This perspective complicates the discourse on the Singularity, urging a balanced view that considers both potential gains and the profound implications of technological power. The work of Sherry Turkle adds a critical dimension to the discussion of human-AI interaction, challenging assumptions about technology as a purely beneficial force. In her seminal work Alone Together, Turkle explores how the encroachment of AI on daily life shapes human relationships and identities, leading to profound social ramifications. She argues that while AI can enhance connectivity, it can also foster isolation and reduce authentic human engagement. Turkle's observations serve as a reminder that the transformation heralded by AI is not solely about intellectual or material advancements; it is equally about the nature of our social fabric and psychological well-being. By highlighting the emotional and relational impacts of AI implementation, Turkle calls for a deeper understanding of what it means to be human in an increasingly automated world. Her insights invite a reevaluation of the societal implications of AI, underscoring the necessity for an interdisciplinary approach to this rapidly evolving domain.

Predictions Surrounding the Singularity

One significant aspect of the discussions surrounding the Singularity involves the potential consequences of achieving superintelligent AI. Advocates of this concept assert that the introduction of machines capable of cognitive functions surpassing those of humans could lead to unparalleled advancements in problem-solving capabilities, effectively addressing many issues that plague humanity today, from climate change to disease eradication. This optimistic vision posits that superintelligent beings will possess not only the capacity to enhance scientific research but also the ability to govern complex systems more effectively than current human institutions. This potential also raises pressing ethical questions: who will control this superintelligent entity, and for what purposes will it be used? The outcomes of deploying such intelligence are contingent upon the motivations and morals of the people orchestrating its development and deployment, suggesting a need for robust frameworks that prioritize the welfare of all stakeholders within society. In contrast, skeptics express caution regarding the unforeseen challenges that may accompany the emergence of superintelligent AI. These critics argue that while advancements in technology could yield significant benefits, they could also lead to catastrophic consequences if not properly regulated. The fear of losing control over intelligent systems stems from historical precedents, where humanity underestimated the risks associated with new technologies, leading to both societal upheaval and environmental degradation. Concerns about the unpredictable nature of AI decision-making and the potential for unintended outcomes echo throughout the discourse. The singularity could exacerbate existing inequalities, as access to advanced AI technologies may become a privilege of the few, further entrenching societal divides. Avoiding such scenarios highlights the urgent need for interdisciplinary collaboration that encompasses ethicists, technologists, policymakers, and various communities to ensure a responsible approach toward intelligent technologies. The discourse surrounding the Singularity often grapples with existential questions about the essence of humanity itself. As machines become increasingly capable of mimicking human cognition and emotions, what distinguishes human identity becomes a contentious issue. Will the advent of superintelligent AI redefine what it means to be human, prompting a reevaluation of our place in the cosmos? Some theorists suggest this evolution could lead to a symbiotic relationship, wherein humans integrate with advanced technologies, enhancing their own cognitive and physical capabilities. This notion, while exciting, is accompanied by profound apprehensions about loss of autonomy and the erasure of fundamental human experiences. Thus, as technological boundaries continue to blur, society must confront its own values and fears, ensuring the narratives we create around AI development align with a vision that respects the complexities of human life while exploring the promising horizons of innovation.

III. TECHNOLOGICAL FOUNDATIONS OF AI

The intricate landscape of AI is built upon several critical technological foundations that enable its capabilities. At the core of AI are algorithms, particularly machine learning and deep learning techniques that allow systems to learn from vast amounts of data. These algorithms mimic the neurological structure of the human brain, utilizing artificial neural networks to process data in ways that enhance efficiency and accuracy. The importance of big data cannot be understated; as AI systems are fed more information, they become better at recognizing patterns and making informed predictions. This relationship between data and algorithm provenance is pivotal in facilitating advancements across diverse sectors, from autonomous vehicles to personalized medicine. Advancements in computational power, such as those provided by Graphics Processing Units (GPUs) and specialized hardware, have allowed complex models to be trained more rapidly, significantly contributing to the explosive growth of AI seen in recent years. Cloud computing has emerged as another cornerstone of AIs technological framework, enabling accessibility and scalability that traditional computing models cannot offer. By housing massive amounts of data and processing power remotely, cloud services have democratized access to AI technologies, enabling even small enterprises to deploy sophisticated AI applications without substantial upfront investments in infrastructure. This shift has not only inspired innovation but has also fostered a collaborative environment where businesses can leverage shared resources.

As companies increasingly utilize cloud platforms, they can continually update their AI models and algorithms, ensuring their systems remain competitive and efficient. This proliferation of AI applications has led to a robust ecosystem of tools and services designed to facilitate AI deployment, further driving the growth and adoption of AI technologies across various domains. Integrating advancements in robotics with AI presents one of the most transformative potentials of these technologies. Robotics, coupled with AI, extends beyond traditional mechanization, allowing machines to not only perform tasks but also adapt and learn in real-time. In industrial settings, AI-driven robots enhance productivity by analyzing data from manufacturing processes to optimize workflows and predict maintenance needs. In sectors like healthcare, robotic systems powered by AI can assist in surgeries, diagnosis, and patient care with precision and analytical depth previously unimaginable. These developments also raise pertinent questions regarding ethics, ensuring that as these technologies evolve, they do so in a manner that promotes human dignity and welfare. As society stands at the brink of what has been termed the Singularity, the integration of AI with robotics challenges us to carefully consider the implications of technology on our lives, emphasizing a need for responsible stewardship as we navigate this pivotal moment in history.

Machine Learning and Deep Learning

The transformation facilitated by advancements in machine learning and deep learning has become undeniable, significantly influencing various sectors from healthcare to finance. Machine learning, as a subset of artificial intelligence, encompasses algorithms that allow computers to learn from and make predictions based on data. It operates on the principle of identifying patterns and leveraging these insights to inform decision-making processes, greatly enhancing efficiency and accuracy. Deep learning, a more specialized area within machine learning, utilizes layered neural networks to process large volumes of unstructured data, such as images and text. This capability enables systems to perform tasks that previously required human intuition, leading to revolutionary changes in how machines are utilized across disciplines. As these technologies continue to mature, their potential to reshape societal frameworks becomes clearer, fostering a ripe environment for innovation and challenging traditional operational methods. Continuing this momentum, the ethical implications and risks associated with machine learning and deep learning are garnering increasing attention. The integration of these technologies into everyday life raises questions about bias, accountability, and the potential for misuse. Algorithms trained on biased data can perpetuate and amplify social inequalities, leading to discriminatory outcomes in areas such as hiring and law enforcement. As machine learning systems gain greater autonomy, the challenge of establishing accountability becomes paramount; it is crucial to determine the responsibility for decisions made by AI. The phenomenon of deepfake technology highlights the potential for these advancements to be utilized maliciously, undermining trust in digital media. As society grapples with these complex ethical dilemmas, a balanced approach that fosters innovation while safeguarding human values is essential for navigating the future. The rapid evolution of machine learning and deep learning also has profound implications for the workforce, prompting discussions about the future role of humans in an increasingly automated world. As these technologies become more adept at performing tasks traditionally carried out by people, there is a growing concern about job displacement and the need for workforce reskilling. While some argue that automation may lead to significant unemployment, others suggest that new job categories will emerge that require distinctly human skills, such as creativity and emotional intelligence. This paradigm shift underscores the importance of embracing lifelong learning and adaptability to remain relevant in a technology-driven landscape. Education systems and corporate training programs must evolve to prepare individuals for this new reality, equipping them with the skills necessary to collaborate with advanced AI systems. The integration of machine learning and deep learning into various industries presents both challenges and opportunities, calling for a proactive societal response to harness the benefits while mitigating the risks.

Neural Networks and Their Functionality

The intricate mechanisms underlying neural networks can be analogized to the structure and functioning of the human brain, where individual neurons communicate through synaptic connections to process information. At their core, neural networks are composed of layers of interconnected nodes, or artificial neurons, each performing simple computations. Inputs are fed into the network, passed through hidden layers where various transformations occur, and culminate in an output layer that delivers the final prediction or classification. This hierarchical arrangement enables the model to learn complex patterns by adjusting the weights of connections based on the data it processes. Through a method known as backpropagation, neural networks iterate on their predictions, gradually refining their operations to minimize error. Consequently, the power of this learning architecture lies not merely in its ability to handle vast amounts of data but also in its capacity for generalization, allowing the model to apply acquired knowledge to novel inputs, a feature crucial for tasks ranging from image recognition to natural language processing. Underlying the effectiveness of neural networks is the principle of activation functions, which introduce non-linearity into the learning process, enabling the model to grasp intricate relationships in data. Common activation functions, such as the sigmoid, ReLU (Rectified Linear Unit), and tanh, dictate how inputs are transformed at each neuron, thereby influencing the overall behavior of the network. These functions enable the model to create complex decision boundaries, distinguishing between varying classes within data. As neural networks gain depth—often comprising numerous hidden

31

layers—they manifest an extraordinary capability to extract hierarchical features from raw data, akin to how humans perceive increasingly abstract concepts. In visual data processing, early layers might recognize basic edges and textures, while deeper layers may identify shapes and ultimately objects. This layered learning process can foster advancements in various fields, including autonomous driving, medical imaging, and voice recognition, thereby illustrating the transformative potential of this technology across different sectors. The journey towards deploying neural networks is not without challenges, particularly regarding issues of interpretability and ethical considerations. Many neural networks operate as black boxes, where the underlying decision-making processes remain obscure, complicating efforts to understand how specific conclusions are reached. This opacity poses significant ethical dilemmas, especially in high-stakes scenarios such as healthcare and criminal justice, where biased data could lead to discriminatory outcomes. As the reliance on these systems grows, it becomes imperative to address such concerns while ensuring that models are not only effective but also equitable. The environmental impact of training large neural networks cannot be overlooked, as energy consumption has surged alongside their complexity. These challenges necessitate a critical examination of how we implement and regulate artificial intelligence, emphasizing the importance of balancing technological advancement with ethical responsibility. Thus, as society moves closer to the potential singularity between AI and human intelligence, the discourse surrounding neural networks must evolve to include ethics, transparency, and sustainability.

The Role of Big Data in AI Development

A considerable factor in the progress of AI hinges upon the vast amounts of data generated daily. As a critical pillar of AI development, big data serves as the fuel for machine learning algorithms, shaping their ability to identify patterns, make predictions, and learn autonomously. The volume, variety, and velocity of data collected from diverse sources—ranging from social media interactions to sensor data in smart devices—provide a robust training environment for AI systems. This dynamic minimizes bias and enhances accuracy, allowing algorithms to adapt in real-time to new information. Consequently, the effective harnessing of big data not only propels AI toward greater sophistication but also addresses variability in real-world applications, ultimately improving the reliability and functionality of these intelligent systems. The synergy between big data and AI catalyzes advancements that impact multiple sectors, thereby revolutionizing business operations and enhancing decision-making processes. Industries from healthcare to finance capitalize on AI technologies derived from big data analytics, leading to improved outcomes and efficiency. Predictive analytics powered by extensive historical health data enables early diagnosis and personalized treatment plans, improving patient care significantly. Similarly, financial institutions leverage big data to analyze real-time market trends and consumer behavior, enhancing risk assessment and investment strategies. By transforming how organizations manage information and resources, the confluence of big data and AI fosters innovation and competitiveness in an increasingly data-driven economy. The growing reliance on big data in AI development entails ethical considerations that cannot be overlooked. As entities collect vast troves of personal and behavioral data, concerns regarding privacy, security, and algorithmic bias come to the forefront. The immense influence wielded by data-driven algorithms necessitates a careful examination of accountability and transparency in their deployment. Ensuring that AI systems uphold ethical standards while processing big data is paramount to prevent the perpetuation of bias and the erosion of public trust. As society progresses toward a future dominated by intelligent technologies, establishing clear frameworks and guidelines for data utilization will be crucial in balancing innovation with the safeguarding of individual rights, fostering a more equitable digital landscape in which AI can evolve responsibly and ethically.

IV. THE ACCELERATION OF AI CAPABILITIES

Emerging technologies have experienced exponential growth, serving as both catalysts and frameworks for the acceleration of AI capabilities. Scholars and technologists alike have noted that advancements in computational power, particularly through innovations in machine learning algorithms, allow AI systems to learn and adapt at unprecedented rates. The advent of deep learning, a specialized form of machine learning, has significantly enhanced AI performance in fields such as natural language processing and computer vision, enabling machines to interpret and analyze data with increasingly complex layers of understanding. The increasing availability of vast datasets has equipped AI with the resources necessary to refine its learning processes continuously. As a result, organizations across industries are harnessing these capabilities to automate tasks, improve decision-making, and enhance predictive analytics, thus reshaping workflows and operational efficiency on a global scale. With rapid enhancements in AI technologies come both transformative opportunities and intricate challenges. Consider the healthcare sector, where AI-driven solutions promise groundbreaking advancements in diagnosis, treatment, and patient care. AI algorithms are capable of analyzing extensive medical data to pinpoint patterns that elude human observers, thereby enabling early detection of diseases such as cancer and infections. Ethical dilemmas arise concerning privacy, data security, and the potential for bias in these AI systems. The dual realities of innovation and concern are underscored by societal apprehensions regarding job displacement and the potential for technology to perpetuate inequalities. This complexity necessitates a dialogue among stakeholders—from technologists to ethicists—to ensure that AI is not merely an engine of productivity but a force for equitable and sustainable progress in society. As AIs capabilities accelerate, so too must our commitment to developing frameworks that govern its ethical deployment. The trajectory of AI development raises critical questions about human identity and societal structure in the face of transformative technological advancements. As machines become better at performing tasks traditionally associated with human intelligence, the line between man and machine blurs, prompting philosophical debates about the essence of consciousness and moral agency. The prospect of achieving General AI—a form of AI that possesses the ability to understand and reason across diverse domains akin to human cognition—invites both excitement and existential concern. Many futurists predict that such capabilities could lead to an era of unparalleled innovation, while others warn of potential risks stemming from loss of control or dependency on autonomous systems. The acceleration of AI capabilities is not merely a question of technological advancement; it challenges humanity to re-evaluate its values, ethics, and the very nature of work and creativity in a world where intelligent machines are ever more integrated into the fabric of daily life.

Exponential Growth of Computing Power

As advancements in computing technology continue to accelerate, the implications for AI are profound. By adhering to Moore's Law—an observation made in 1965 noting that the number of transistors on a microchip doubles approximately every two years—scientists and technologists have witnessed unprecedented enhancements in processing ability. This dramatic increase in computing power allows for more complex algorithms to be developed, significantly enhancing AIs capacity to learn and function autonomously. Data that once took hours to process can now be analyzed in real-time, leading to breakthroughs in various fields, including healthcare, finance, and transportation. The enhanced ability to manipulate large datasets not only fosters innovation but also raises pertinent questions about the ethical applications of such technologies and their socio-economic impacts on the workforce and society as a whole. Significantly, the exponential growth of computing power opens the door to new paradigms of machine learning and deep learning. Algorithms designed to mimic cognitive functions have become increasingly sophisticated, enabling programs to perform tasks that were once considered uniquely human. Advancements in neural networks have revolutionized natural language processing, leading to the development of conversational agents that can engage seamlessly with users. This kind of progress suggests that the distinction between human and machine capabilities is narrowing, challenging our understanding of intelligence itself. The accessibility of cloud computing platforms democratizes these technologies, allowing startups and established enterprises alike to harness vast computing resources—

accelerating innovation cycles and creating a fertile environment for technological breakthroughs. This rapid proliferation of computing power and AI technologies invites scrutiny about ethical considerations, particularly regarding data privacy, algorithmic bias, and the implications of replacing human judgment in critical decision-making processes. The societal ramifications of this exponential growth in computing power extend beyond mere technological advancement; they impact the very fabric of human existence. As AI systems become more integrated into daily life, individuals may find themselves increasingly reliant on these tools for personal and professional decision-making. While such reliance can lead to enhanced efficiencies and improved quality of life, it also raises concerns about autonomy and the potential for diminished human agency. The rapid evolution of AI presents a dual-edged sword: on one hand, it holds the promise of solving complex global challenges, such as climate change and disease management; It poses existential risks, including job displacement and ethical dilemmas surrounding accountability and governance. Consequently, society must engage in critical dialogues about the trajectory of these technologies, striving for a balanced approach that recognizes both the potential benefits and the inherent dangers of an increasingly AI-driven world. The ongoing discourse will be instrumental in shaping norms and regulations that can guide the ethical deployment of these transformative technologies.

Advances in Algorithms and Software

The evolution of algorithms has significantly shaped the capabilities of artificial intelligence, particularly in its application to real-world problems. Early algorithms were primarily rule-based and limited in scope, relying heavily on human input to design and implement problem-solving procedures. Advancements in machine learning, particularly through deep learning techniques, have introduced algorithms that can self-optimize and adapt based on large datasets. This transformative capability has enabled AI systems to identify patterns and make predictions with unprecedented accuracy, revolutionizing industries from healthcare to finance. Algorithms can now analyze medical images for early signs of disease, providing diagnostic support that was once solely dependent on human expertise. The implications of these developments extend beyond mere efficiency; they raise critical questions about reliance on algorithmic decision-making and the potential for biases inherent in training data. As these advanced algorithms become integral to decision-making processes, the challenge lies in ensuring transparency and accountability in their applications. The software architectures that support modern algorithms have also undergone substantial transformation, facilitating greater complexity and versatility in AI systems. Frameworks such as TensorFlow and PyTorch have democratized access to sophisticated machine learning capabilities, empowering developers and researchers alike to build and deploy their own AI models. The modular nature of these platforms allows for the integration of various components, enabling the seamless application of different algorithms to solve diverse problems. Cloud computing has significantly altered the software landscape, allowing for massive data processing and storage solutions that were previously unattainable for many organizations. This convergence of powerful software and scalable infrastructure is accelerating innovation and adoption of AI technologies across sectors, as businesses leverage these tools to enhance productivity and create more personalized consumer experiences. Yet, this abundance of computational power also raises critical considerations regarding data privacy and the ethical implications of AI deployment, as organizations must navigate the fine line between leveraging technology for advancement and safeguarding individual rights. Looking forward, the synergy between advances in algorithms and software technology poses both opportunities and challenges that will define the future of AI and its role in human transformation. As algorithms continue to evolve, they increasingly require sophisticated software environments to harness their full potential, leading to a reciprocal relationship between these two domains. Emerging concepts, such as federated learning, illustrate the innovative approaches scholars are exploring to enhance learning while preserving data privacy, highlighting the necessity of ethics in algorithm development. As AI systems become more autonomous, questions surrounding the interpretation and accountability of their decisions must be rigorously addressed, given the potential consequences on societal structures. The path to a future dominated by AI hinges on careful consideration of not just technological capabilities, but also the ethical frameworks that govern their application, ensuring that humanity remains at the center of this transformative journey toward the singularity.

The Impact of Quantum Computing

In recent years, the emergence of quantum computing has elicited both excitement and apprehension, profoundly influencing our understanding of computational limits. Unlike classical computers, which rely on bits as the smallest units of data that can be either 0 or 1, quantum computers utilize qubits that can exist in multiple states simultaneously thanks to the principles of superposition and entanglement. This revolutionary capability allows quantum machines to perform complex calculations at speeds unattainable by conventional systems. Problems such as factorizing large integers or simulating molecular structures, foundational to many scientific inquiries including drug discovery and materials science, can potentially be solved exponentially faster. The integration of quantum computing into various sectors is positioned not merely as an enhancement of existing technologies but as a paradigm shift, pushing boundaries that were previously considered impenetrable. As these developments unfold, they prompt vital discussions about the implications for both technological progress and ethical considerations. The potential benefits of quantum computing are juxtaposed with significant concerns regarding security and ethical responsibilities. Traditional encryption methods, which underpin much of our digital security, could become obsolete due to the capabilities of quantum algorithms, such as Shor's algorithm, designed to decrypt RSA encryption with remarkable efficiency. This shift could expose sensitive personal and national data to unprecedented vulnerabilities, prompting urgent calls for the development of quantum-resistant encryption methods. The disparity in access to quantum technology raises ethical dilemmas

41

about who will control these powerful tools and how they will be used. The potential for quantum technologies to exacerbate existing inequalities is worrisome, as nations or corporations with advanced capabilities could leverage these tools for strategic advantages. Thus, as society stands on the brink of a quantum leap, it becomes imperative to instigate frameworks that ensure equitable access and governance of this transformative technology to mitigate risks associated with its misuse. The integration of quantum computing into the broader sphere of technology could significantly reshape the landscape of artificial intelligence. The ability to process vast amounts of data more rapidly could enhance machine learning algorithms, allowing AI systems to learn and adapt more efficiently and accurately. This interplay between quantum computing and AI presents opportunities to tackle complex problems beyond our current reach, ranging from climate modeling to personalized medicine. Yet, this rapid advancement necessitates a cautious approach, as the dual-use nature of these technologies can lead to both beneficial applications and detrimental consequences. A proactive stance on regulatory measures and ethical considerations is essential to ensure that the convergence of quantum and AI technologies aligns with human values and goals. As society navigates the intricate tapestry of progress, harnessing the potential of quantum computing while managing its implications will be crucial in shaping a future that prioritizes well-being and progress for all.

V. AI IN EVERYDAY LIFE

In recent years, the integration of AI into daily life has become increasingly tangible, revolutionizing how individuals interact with technology. From voice-activated virtual assistants to personalized content recommendations, AI is embedding itself into the fabric of routine activities. These advancements allow for a level of convenience and efficiency previously unimaginable, as tasks ranging from scheduling appointments to managing household activities are streamlined through intelligent systems. The constant accessibility of AI-infused applications not only enhances productivity but also fosters a dependency on these technologies, prompting individuals to reevaluate their understanding of autonomy and control in an age defined by digital assistance. The impact of AI extends beyond mere convenience; it deeply influences social and economic landscapes. Businesses harness machine learning algorithms to optimize services, enhance customer experiences, and anticipate consumer behavior, creating a competitive edge in increasingly crowded markets. This technological reliance can be seen in diverse sectors, such as healthcare, where AI diagnostics can lead to more accurate and timely patient care, or in the automotive industry, which is making strides toward the mainstream adoption of autonomous vehicles. As organizations seek to leverage AI capabilities, concerns about data privacy, job displacement, and ethical considerations emerge, urging a critical dialogue about responsible innovation and the need for regulatory frameworks to mitigate potential risks associated with widespread AI adoption. As individuals navigate their increasingly AI-enhanced environments, the dialogue around personal ethics and societal norms becomes paramount. With every advancement comes the responsibility to critically examine the implications of integrating AI into everyday life. The convenience offered by these technologies often overshadows the ethical dilemmas they may present, such as issues of surveillance, consent, and algorithmic bias. In fostering a dialogue about these concerns, society must also cultivate an awareness of the potential long-term consequences of AI domination, including the risk of exacerbating social inequalities and eroding fundamental human skills. A balanced approach is essential, one that embraces the advantages of AI while remaining vigilant about its capacity to disrupt traditional human experiences and relationships. Through mindful engagement with AI, individuals and communities can navigate this transformative period and shape a future where technology serves humanity's best interests.

Integration of AI in Consumer Products

Consumer products have witnessed a significant evolution with the advent of AI technologies, which are increasingly embedding intelligent functionalities into everyday items. Through the integration of machine learning and data analytics, manufacturers are creating products that not only react to user inputs but also learn and adapt to individual behaviors over time. Smart home devices such as thermostats and lighting systems are now equipped with AI that allows them to assess patterns in daily routines. This results in automated adjustments that enhance convenience, conserve energy, and create personalized environments. As a result, the incorporation of AI into these products not only improves usability but also fosters a deeper engagement between users and their environments, contributing to a seamless interaction between technology and daily life. The embedding of AI in consumer products extends beyond mere functionality; it raises critical ethical questions surrounding privacy and data security. Many AI-driven devices collect vast amounts of personal and behavioral data to optimize performance, leading to concerns about who has access to this information and how it is used. Voice-activated assistants gather audio snippets that can potentially be stored and analyzed by third parties, raising the specter of unauthorized surveillance and data exploitation. The transparency of algorithms employed in these devices remains obscured to the average user, complicating the issue of accountability. As consumers increasingly rely on AI-enhanced products, it is essential for manufacturers to prioritize ethical standards that safeguard privacy and fortify trust, lest they compromise the very benefits that AI integration aims to provide. The transformative potential of AI in consumer products is undeniable, yet achieving a balance between innovation and ethical responsibility is paramount. As these technologies evolve, regulatory frameworks may need to be established to ensure that advancements serve the public good without endangering individual rights. Companies must engage in proactive dialogues with consumers about the implications of their products, fostering an environment where users are not only informed but also empowered to make choices based on their values. The development of AI products should consider inclusivity and accessibility, ensuring that all segments of society can benefit from technological advancements. In this landscape, the ultimate goal must transcend profitability; it should be rooted in the vision of enhancing human well-being and societal progress, harnessing the transformative capabilities of AI while respecting the foundational tenets of ethical governance.

AI in Healthcare and Medicine

Advancements in AI are fundamentally reshaping healthcare by streamlining diagnostic processes and personalizing treatment plans. As AI technologies analyze vast amounts of medical data, they uncover patterns that may elude even the most experienced clinicians. Platforms powered by machine learning can identify subtle indicators of diseases like cancer in imaging scans with remarkable accuracy, thereby facilitating early intervention. AI algorithms can process genetic information and patient history to propose tailored therapies, optimizing outcomes for individuals. Such innovations not only enhance the quality of care but also address the issue of resource scarcity in healthcare systems, allowing practitioners to focus on more complex cases, thus augmenting the human element of patient care. Collaboration between AI systems and healthcare professionals fosters an environment where human insight and machine efficiency coexist. AI does not seek to replace human practitioners but rather to augment their capabilities, enabling them to leverage extensive databases and predictive models in real time. This symbiotic relationship encourages healthcare providers to engage in data-driven decision-making, enhancing accuracy and reducing the likelihood of errors. While AI can suggest probable diagnoses based on patient symptoms, it is ultimately the healthcare professional who processes this information through a compassionate lens, taking into account the emotional and psychological aspects of patient interaction. This integration not only refines diagnostic accuracy but also enriches the therapeutic alliance between patients and providers, ensuring a holistic approach to health and well-being. Despite its promising potential, the deployment of AI in healthcare raises critical ethical questions and concerns regarding patient privacy and data security. As personal health data is increasingly used to feed AI systems, ensuring stringent safeguards becomes paramount to protect against breaches and misuse. The reliance on algorithms that may inadvertently perpetuate biases raises the risk of health disparities among various demographic groups. It is essential for stakeholders – from technologists to healthcare professionals and policymakers – to collaborate in establishing robust ethical frameworks as AI technologies continue to evolve. Achieving balance in harnessing AIs advantages while addressing these concerns is fundamental to facilitating its integration into healthcare, thereby ensuring that the transformation brought about by AI serves humanity positively and equitably.

AI's Role in Education and Learning

In an era marked by rapid technological advancements, the integration of AI into educational frameworks offers unprecedented opportunities for personalized learning experiences. Tailoring educational content to meet individual needs, AI-driven platforms can analyze a student's strengths and weaknesses, subsequently recommending resources that are finely tuned to their learning styles. Adaptive learning technologies utilize machine learning algorithms to adjust the difficulty level of tasks in real-time, ensuring students remain engaged and adequately challenged. These capabilities not only enhance traditional learning processes but also democratize education by providing access to high-quality resources and instruction tailored to diverse learning paces, thereby promoting inclusivity. The implementation of AI in education necessitates a careful examination of its implications, particularly concerning data privacy and the potential biases embedded within AI algorithms, underscoring the importance of ethical considerations in deploying such technologies. The role of AI extends beyond personalized learning pathways; it also enhances administrative efficiencies within educational institutions. AI systems can optimize scheduling, track student attendance, and facilitate resource allocation, alleviating the bureaucratic burdens that often hinder institutional effectiveness. By streamlining these processes, administrators are afforded more time to focus on fostering a nurturing educational environment and implementing pedagogical innovations. AI-powered analytics provide administrators with actionable insights into student performance, allowing for data-driven decisions that can enhance curricula and instructional strategies.

With these advancements comes a challenge: the necessity for educators to adapt to an evolving technological landscape. Professional development and training become pivotal in ensuring that educators are proficient in leveraging AI tools to support their teaching, thereby encouraging a collaborative relationship between educators and technology in the classroom. The intersection of AI and education redefines both teaching methodologies and learning outcomes, ushering in an era where students can become architects of their own educational journeys. With AI facilitating an interactive and immersive learning environment, students are encouraged to engage with material in dynamic and meaningful ways. This shift not only promotes critical thinking and problem-solving skills but also cultivates a sense of agency among learners, as they navigate through personalized educational paths. Nonetheless, as education systems begin to fully integrate AI, it is crucial to balance technological advancements with the cultivation of humanistic values in education. The future landscape of learning must embrace not only AIs capabilities but also the social and emotional aspects of education, ensuring that students emerge not only as technologically adept individuals but also as empathetic and socially conscious members of society. The responsible incorporation of AI in education has the potential to significantly enrich the learning experience while also acknowledging the ethical obligations inherent in shaping the future of education.

VI. ECONOMIC IMPLICATIONS OF AI

The integration of AI into various sectors fundamentally alters traditional economic structures and paradigms. As AI systems become increasingly sophisticated, labor market dynamics are undergoing significant shifts. Automation is poised to displace certain manual labor and routine cognitive tasks, leading to potential job losses in sectors such as manufacturing, retail, and even services like customer support. This displacement also presents opportunities for economic growth by creating new jobs in AI design, implementation, and maintenance, which require different skill sets. These changes could increase the demand for higher education and vocational training, compelling a workforce transition that emphasizes continuous learning and adaptability. Striking a balance between mitigating unemployment and leveraging innovation presents a critical challenge for policymakers aiming to harness AIs economic benefits while protecting vulnerable workers. There is also a transformative effect of AI on productivity and economic efficiency that cannot be overlooked. Businesses leveraging AI technologies can optimize supply chain management, enhance customer experiences through targeted marketing, and improve decision-making with data-driven insights. This increased efficiency leads to lower operational costs and the potential for higher profit margins, fundamentally altering competitive dynamics within and across industries. The integration of AI into economic processes can lead to greater output with fewer resources, driving economic growth on a macroeconomic level. This could result in an uneven distribution of economic gains. Companies that successfully adopt AI technologies may experience substantial benefits, while those unable or unwilling to adapt may face declines, further exacerbating income inequality and leading to economic polarization. The implications of AI extend beyond individual sectors and businesses, influencing broader economic policy and societal structures. Governments are tasked with addressing the economic consequences of AI, which necessitates a reevaluation of regulatory frameworks and social safety nets. Policymakers must consider the implications of AI on taxation, employment insurance, and retraining programs to ensure that all citizens can benefit from technological advancements. Addressing ethical concerns related to data privacy, algorithmic bias, and the potential for monopolistic behavior in AI development is crucial in fostering a fair economic landscape. The transition into an AI-driven economy requires a collaborative approach, where public and private sectors work together to create policies that promote responsible innovation while also ensuring equitable access to the benefits of AI, thus preparing society for an inevitable shift in the economic landscape.

Job Displacement and Creation

The landscape of employment is undergoing profound shifts driven by technological advancements, particularly in artificial intelligence. The transformation is multifaceted, with significant sectors experiencing both job displacement and the emergence of new roles. Routine and manual tasks are increasingly performed by machines, which threaten traditional positions in manufacturing, retail, and administrative sectors. As AI systems gain proficiency in data analysis and customer interaction, roles that once required a human touch are rapidly being automated. While this evolution fosters economic efficiency, it also introduces substantial challenges for workers who find themselves grappling with obsolescence. Education and training must adapt to prepare individuals for an evolving job market where analytical skills and technological proficiency are paramount, ensuring that the workforce remains resilient amid change. Conversely, the rise of AI and advanced technologies heralds the creation of entirely new job categories, signifying that while some jobs may vanish, others will materialize, designed to harness the capabilities of these innovations. Sectors such as AI development, cybersecurity, and renewable energy technology are expanding, demanding a diverse range of expertise. As businesses integrate automated systems, the need for professionals who can design, implement, and maintain these technologies becomes critical. The growing emphasis on AI ethics and policy suggests an opportunity for roles focused on ensuring that the deployment of such technologies aligns with societal values. This duality of job displacement and creation underscores the importance of adaptability; workers equipped with the ability to learn and re-skill will be more likely to thrive in this new employment landscape. The interaction of displacing and creating jobs within the context of AI advancements presents both opportunities and challenges. Societal adaptation hinges not solely on individual resilience, but also on comprehensive policy frameworks designed to facilitate smooth transitions between displaced workers and emerging job opportunities. Technical education initiatives, upskilling programs, and social safety nets can serve to mitigate the impacts of job loss while preparing the workforce for the opportunities on the horizon. Engaging with stakeholders from diverse sectors—government, industry, and educational institutions—will enhance collaborative efforts to shape policies that support inclusive growth in the face of technological disruption. The balance between job displacement and creation must be continually assessed to foster a future where AI complements human capabilities rather than undermines them, ensuring that advancements benefit all strata of society.

Changes in Industry Dynamics

The rapid integration of AI into various industries has fundamentally altered the operational landscape, prompting a closer examination of evolving business practices. Companies are increasingly adopting AI-driven technologies within their organizational frameworks to enhance productivity, improve decision-making, and optimize resource allocation. This shift, Is not merely a trend; it reflects a deeper metamorphosis in how industries interact with technology. By leveraging data analytics and machine learning, businesses can gain insights that were previously inaccessible, allowing them to adapt swiftly to market changes. While this creates opportunities for innovation and growth, it also poses significant challenges, particularly for traditional entities that may struggle to keep pace with the transformations. The disparity between those who embrace these advancements and those who resist can create a stratified market, necessitating a reevaluation of business strategies across the spectrum of industry stakeholders. The competitive landscape is undergoing a profound restructuring due to these technological advancements, leading to heightened market volatility. Industry leaders that harness AIs capabilities are finding themselves at a distinct advantage, capable of responding with agility to consumer demands and global trends. This dynamism fosters an arms race for technological superiority, where companies invest heavily in research and development to maintain their edge. The implications of this race are multifaceted; not only do they accelerate innovation cycles, but they also increase the risk of obsolescence for businesses unable to adapt. As industries reconfigure around AI, the roles of human labor and expertise are also in contention, raising questions about the future of employment and the skills necessary for the workforce. Companies after investing in AI must also consider the ethical dimensions of automation, balancing efficiency with the human cost involved. These transformations bear significant implications for the overall economy and society at large. As businesses pivot to AI-centric models, the potential for significant job displacement looms large, prompting discussions about the need for retraining and reskilling initiatives. There exists a growing consciousness about the ethical considerations intertwined with such changes—issues such as data privacy, algorithmic bias, and the implications of decision-making algorithms can raise concerns about equitable access and fairness. While AI holds promise for economic growth and societal advancement, its integration must be approached with caution, ensuring that the benefits are widely distributed. As industries continually adapt to these technological shifts, a collaborative dialogue among stakeholders—including policymakers, business leaders, and the workforce—will be essential in crafting a future that acknowledges, mitigates, and strategically manages the risks while maximizing the rewards associated with these seismic changes in industry dynamics.

The Future of Work in an AI-Driven Economy

As we transition into an era dominated by artificial intelligence, the landscape of employment is undergoing profound transformation. The integration of AI technologies is not merely an enhancement of existing job functions; it represents a fundamental shift in the nature of work itself. Routine tasks that demand minimal cognitive effort—such as data entry and basic customer service—are increasingly being automated. The crux of this evolution lies in job displacement versus job creation. While some positions may vanish, new roles are emerging in fields such as AI programming, data analysis, and machine maintenance. This necessitates a reevaluation of educational and vocational training, aiming to equip the workforce with skills that are complementary to AI rather than competing against it. This shift informs not only economic policies but also individual career trajectories, emphasizing adaptability and lifelong learning as essential qualities in the contemporary job market. Central to the dialogue surrounding the future of work is the need for a cultural shift in how society perceives labor and productivity. As AI systems assume a greater share of routine and repetitive tasks, questions arise about the meaning and value of human work. It is essential to recognize that the emotional and creative dimensions of labor remain uniquely human traits that cannot easily be replicated by machines. Professions heavily reliant on human interaction—such as healthcare, education, and the arts—are likely to thrive in this AI-driven economy, as they require empathy, intuition, and creativity. Redefining success in these terms challenges traditional metrics of productivity and encourages a wholesale rethinking of job satisfaction and fulfillment. In this context, individuals may pursue careers that resonate more profoundly with their values and aspirations, paving the way for a workforce that prioritizes purpose over mere economic gain. The trajectory toward an AI-centric workforce raises significant ethical and social challenges that must be confronted. Issues of equity come into play when considering who has access to the skills and training necessary to thrive in this new landscape. The risk of deepening socioeconomic divides becomes pronounced if educational opportunities remain concentrated among privileged populations, leaving marginalized communities further behind. The psychological effects of job displacement on workers must be navigated carefully. As traditional employment models shift dramatically, comprehensive support systems, including retraining programs and mental health resources, will be vital. Policymakers and organizations must collaborate to create frameworks that not only foster technological innovation but also promote a fair distribution of its benefits across society. The future of work, Hinges not merely on technological advances but also on our collective commitment to building an inclusive, resilient workforce capable of adapting to these seismic changes.

VII. ETHICAL CONSIDERATIONS

As advancements in AI surge forward, the ethical implications surrounding its integration into society become increasingly pressing. The potential for misuse of AI technologies raises significant concerns about privacy and surveillance. With powerful algorithms capable of analyzing vast amounts of data, there is an inherent risk that personal information could be exploited, leading to violations of human rights. The ability of AI to predict human behavior through data analytics can erode notions of autonomy and consent. These considerations demand that developers and policymakers establish strict guidelines and frameworks for ethical usage. The fundamental challenge lies not only in harnessing AI's capabilities for societal benefit but also in safeguarding individual rights and maintaining public trust in these emerging technologies. Striking the right balance is paramount to preventing dystopian scenarios that could arise from the unchecked proliferation of AI systems. Implications of bias are another critical aspect of the ethical conversation surrounding AI. Often, algorithms are trained on datasets that reflect historical inequities, inadvertently perpetuating discrimination in decision-making processes across various sectors, including hiring, law enforcement, and finance. When AI systems are not scrutinized for bias, the consequences can be dire—certain groups may be unfairly targeted or overlooked, reinforcing social disparities rather than alleviating them. Addressing these biases involves a multi-faceted approach, encompassing the diversification of datasets, rigorous testing across demographic lines, and inclusive team dynamics in AI development. Such measures will enable the creation of fairer and more representative AI systems. Importantly, ethical AI development must extend beyond mere compliance with regulations; it should be guided by principles of justice and equity, ensuring that the advantages of these technologies are widely shared and do not exacerbate existing societal divides. The existential risks associated with AI development prompt urgent ethical discussions that transcend immediate practicalities. As machines grow more intelligent, considerations surrounding autonomy and decision-making emerge. The potential for AI systems to surpass human capabilities poses profound questions regarding control and accountability. If an autonomous vehicle is involved in an accident, determining culpability becomes complicated, challenging traditional notions of responsibility. The prospect of AI systems making critical decisions—ranging from life-saving medical interventions to military applications—raises concerns about the moral implications of entrusting machines with human lives. This calls for a reassessment of ethical frameworks that govern AI, emphasizing transparency and the need for human oversight. Only through a holistic understanding of these existential questions can society hope to navigate the perilous landscape of technological advancement while preserving ethical integrity.

Moral Implications of AI Decision-Making

The advent of AI has prompted a re-evaluation of our ethical frameworks, particularly in the domain of decision-making. Traditionally, moral decisions have been grounded in human experience, empathy, and accountability. As algorithms take over more complex decision-making roles—from healthcare diagnostics to criminal justice sentencing—they challenge our understanding of moral agency. The opacity of AI systems complicates this further, as the lack of transparency surrounding their decision-making processes can obscure accountability. In cases where an AI system makes a harmful decision, identifying responsibility becomes muddled, raising profound questions about the ethical implications of delegating moral choices to machines. This shift necessitates a reconsideration of existing ethical frameworks or the potential development of new ones engineered specifically to guide AI behavior, aiming to ensure that technological progress does not outpace our moral capacities. Examining the moral implications of AI decision-making also compels a critical dialogue around bias and fairness. AI systems are trained on data sets that reflect existing human biases—whether they pertain to race, gender, or socioeconomic status—which can be perpetuated and even amplified by algorithmic decision-making. This creates an ethical dilemma: how do we govern technologies that can inadvertently reinforce systemic inequalities? The stakes are particularly high in contexts such as hiring practices, where algorithmic tools can filter candidates based on biased historical data, thereby entrenching inequality and eroding trust in societal institutions. Addressing this issue requires not only enhanced vigilance in the development and deployment of AI technology but also comprehensive retraining of algorithms to include fairness as a critical metric. Only through these proactive measures can we hope to align AIs capabilities with our core values of justice and equity, ensuring that advancements benefit all members of society rather than perpetuating existing disparities. The implications of AI decision-making extend beyond technical challenges; they compel us to confront fundamental questions about the nature of morality itself. As humans increasingly coexist with intelligent systems, we must grapple with the philosophical ramifications of such entanglements. If AI can make decisions at a level of cognitive sophistication comparable to humans, what does that mean for our understanding of agency, responsibility, and the essence of human judgement? This intersection of technology and moral philosophy fosters a landscape where traditional human-centric ethical frameworks might be insufficient. Consequently, engaging in interdisciplinary dialogues across ethics, technology, and law will be vital for crafting a future where AI operates within a moral context aligned with human values. Only then can we hope to navigate the complex terrain of human transformation in the age of AI, ensuring it serves to enhance rather than diminish our collective moral fabric.

Privacy Concerns and Data Security

Advancements in AI are fundamentally altering the nature of data collection and processing, raising profound questions regarding individual privacy. As technology companies increasingly harness vast amounts of personal information, the line between convenience and intrusion blurs significantly. AI systems can analyze social media behavior, browsing histories, and consumer preferences, constructing detailed digital profiles of users. These profiles not only serve targeted advertising but also facilitate predictive analytics that can influence how services and products are marketed. The result is a landscape where personal data is commodified, often without users' informed consent, prompting serious ethical dilemmas about one's right to privacy in an era of omnipresent surveillance. As society embraces the efficiencies offered by these technologies, the implicit trade-off becomes the erosion of personal autonomy, calling for a critical examination of the systems designed to protect individual privacy. The intersection of AI and data security creates significant vulnerabilities that can lead to potential abuses. As cyberattacks become more sophisticated, threatening both public and private institutions, the security of sensitive personal data is increasingly jeopardized. High-profile breaches have demonstrated that even the most robust security measures can falter against determined attackers, resulting in personal information falling into the wrong hands. This situation underscores the inherent risks associated with the extensive data accumulation necessary for AI algorithms to function effectively. The consequences of such breaches extend beyond financial losses; they can severely impact individuals' lives, with identity theft, financial fraud, and privacy violations wreaking havoc on victims. Protecting data security thus becomes paramount, not only as a technical challenge but also as a societal imperative to preserve the trust necessary for continued innovation in AI technologies. Addressing the dual challenges of privacy concerns and data security requires a multifaceted approach that includes regulatory frameworks, technological safeguards, and increased public awareness. Governments must implement comprehensive data protection laws that prioritize individuals rights while holding organizations accountable for data management practices. The General Data Protection Regulation (GDPR) in Europe serves as a model that enforces strict guidelines on data handling and necessitates transparency in how user data is collected and utilized. Organizations should invest in advanced security measures and develop ethical AI frameworks that proactively mitigate risks. This holistic strategy must also engage the public, educating individuals about their rights and the implications of their digital footprints in an AI-driven world. Safeguarding privacy in the age of AI is not merely a technical issue but a fundamental human right that must be championed if society is to reap the benefits of technological advancements without sacrificing individual freedom.

The Challenge of Bias in AI Systems

Unequal representation in data can lead to significant complications in the functionality of AI systems. In many cases, the datasets used to train AI models contain biases that reflect historical and societal inequities. Consider facial recognition software that is trained predominantly on images of lighter-skinned individuals; the resulting algorithm may misidentify or fail to recognize individuals with darker skin tones, perpetuating harmful stereotypes and discrimination against marginalized groups. This confluence of biased training data and AI deployment can exacerbate existing disparities rather than ameliorate them. As AI systems are increasingly deployed in sensitive areas like hiring, law enforcement, and loan approvals, the ramifications of these biases become critical. Organizations must recognize that their pursuit of technological advancement must be tempered by a commitment to ethical responsibility, ensuring their algorithms do not replicate or worsen social injustices. Addressing the challenge of bias in AI systems demands a concerted effort across various sectors, from academia to industry to government. Implementing ethical AI practices requires collaboration between technologists, ethicists, and affected communities to create guidelines that prioritize fairness and transparency. One solution lies in diversifying data collection methods and employing algorithms that can adapt to prevent biased outcomes. Techniques such as differential privacy and fairness constraints can be integrated into machine learning models to create systems that are more equitable. Organizations can benefit from conducting regular audits of their AI systems to identify and remedy bias before deployment. The integration of interdisciplinary insights will not only enhance the quality and performance of AI applications but also help to build public trust and mitigate the potential backlash against technological innovations perceived as discriminatory. Addressing bias is not merely a technical challenge; it is deeply intertwined with broader ethical considerations and societal implications. The quest for impartiality in AI development raises fundamental questions about accountability and ownership. If AI systems cause harm or perpetuate bias, who is responsible? Is it the developers, the companies deploying the technology, or the regulatory bodies overseeing its implementation? These questions underscore the necessity for robust governance frameworks that prioritize ethical standards. Engaging in public dialogues about the implications of biased AI can foster greater awareness and inclusion of diverse perspectives in technology development. As the reliance on AI grows in everyday life, integrating ethical considerations into the fabric of AI systems will be crucial for ensuring that they contribute to a just and equitable society as humanity navigates the complex terrain of technological transformation.

VIII. AI AND HUMAN IDENTITY

As societies integrate advanced AI into everyday life, a profound inquiry into the essence of human identity emerges. One pertinent consideration is the role of consciousness and subjective experience in distinguishing human beings from machines. While AI systems exhibit remarkable capabilities in data processing, pattern recognition, and even creative tasks, they lack the intrinsic awareness that characterizes the human experience. This absence of consciousness raises philosophical questions: Can an entity without self-awareness truly possess an identity? The very notion of identity is rooted in lived experience, emotions, and the complexities of personal narrative—elements that AI, by its current design, cannot genuinely embody. Thus, while AI presents an impressive imitation of human-like behaviors, it does not and perhaps cannot replace the intricate subtleties of human identity shaped by emotions, memories, and interpersonal relationships. In the face of such technological advancements, the concept of identity inevitably undergoes transformation as humans increasingly interact with AI. This relationship shifts the boundaries of what it means to be human, as individuals find themselves reassessing their roles and self-perceptions in a world where machines can replicate tasks once thought to require human intuition. As tasks become automated, the fear of obsolescence can engender a crisis of identity in individuals who define themselves by their work or social roles. This phenomenon is further compounded by the potential for AI to create personalized systems that may mirror and even enhance individual traits, blurring the line between human and machine. In this milieu, self-definition no longer hinges solely on essential characteristics but on evolving interactions with AI systems, which may ultimately redefine the parameters of human identity itself. The intersection of AI and human identity demands a reevaluation of ethical considerations surrounding this transformative relationship. As AI technologies advance, the potential for their misuse poses questions about the implications for personal autonomy and agency. Should AI systems evolve to the point of influencing human thought or behavior, the risk arises of diminished individuality as people conform to AI-driven expectations or biases. Such concerns prompt critical discourse on the moral responsibility tech developers hold in ensuring their creations enhance rather than undermine human dignity. This dialogue is indispensable in an age when the anthropocentric view of identity is challenged. Addressing these ethical dilemmas not only fosters a deeper understanding of identity within a technologically evolving landscape but also reinforces the necessity of preserving humanity's core values amid rapid change, ensuring that the evolution of human identity continues to prioritize the complexities that make us inherently human.

Redefining Human Capabilities

Advancements in AI are not merely enhancing human capabilities; they are fundamentally reshaping the very definitions of what it means to be human. As AI systems become increasingly sophisticated, they can accomplish tasks that were once considered exclusively within the purview of human intellect, such as complex problem solving and creativity. This leads to a reexamination of our cognitive boundaries, with machines performing roles ranging from medical diagnostics to creative arts. By enhancing our abilities rather than replacing them, these technologies encourage a symbiotic relationship whereby human intuition and emotion can guide AI's analytical prowess. The integration of AI into daily life results in a collaborative enhancement rather than a definitive replacement, shifting our understanding of intelligence and capability. This transformation raises fundamental questions about identity, but it also opens new avenues for cooperation that can potentially lead to richer, more fulfilled lives. Redefining capabilities brings to light the ethical implications of our reliance on artificial intelligence. As AI systems begin to surpass human performance in various fields, society faces dilemmas about dependency, privacy, and decision-making authority. The potential for biases embedded within algorithms can lead to unjust outcomes, highlighting the importance of ethical oversight in AI development and deployment. The challenge of ensuring that AI reflects diverse perspectives while remaining free from prejudice and discrimination becomes critical as technology becomes increasingly pervasive. At the same time, ethical considerations must also address the implications of enhanced capabilities for marginalized groups who may benefit disproportionately from these advancements. By critically analyzing who gets access to these technologies and determining the societal norms governing their use, we can work towards an equitable future where the benefits of AI are shared broadly rather than concentrated among a select few. The reevaluation of human capabilities also presents a unique opportunity for personal growth and societal transformation. As AI augments our physical and cognitive abilities, it creates new paradigms for lifelong learning and adaptation. Individuals are encouraged to rethink their skill sets in light of rapidly advancing technologies, prompting shifts in educational systems, job markets, and even cultural narratives surrounding success and achievement. New avenues for creativity, collaboration, and problem-solving emerge as humans learn to coexist with machines that can enhance their potential. This means that adaptability becomes a critical skill in itself, as individuals must embrace change and uncertainty in their personal and professional lives. Thus, the dialogue around redefining human capabilities is not solely about what technologies can do but revolves around how these advancements can empower us to redefine our aspirations, choices, and Our place in the world.

The Concept of Transhumanism

One of the most provocative aspects of modern technological discourse is the ambition to enhance the human condition beyond its biological limits. Rooted in the concept of transhumanism, this aspiration is fueled by advancements in biotechnology, artificial intelligence, and nanotechnology. Proponents argue that these innovations herald a future where humans can transcend traditional physical and mental constraints, potentially leading to enhanced cognitive abilities, increased lifespan, and improved physical health. Advocates envision a world in which people can eliminate suffering and significantly augment their capabilities. This vision is not without its critics, who warn of the societal implications and ethical dilemmas that arise from the attempt to redefine what it means to be human. The desire for enhanced existence brings forth questions regarding equity, access, and the potential consequences for those unable or unwilling to participate in such enhancements. Skepticism surrounding transhumanism often centers on the ethical ramifications of creating a bifurcated society, one where enhanced individuals may dominate over those who remain grounded in their biological origins. This raises pressing concerns about inequality and potential discrimination based on enhanced versus non-enhanced status. Critics argue that societal structures may evolve to favor genetically or technologically enhanced individuals, leading to a new form of elitism that exacerbates existing socioeconomic divides. The potential loss of human qualities, such as empathy, compassion, and social connection, can pose existential risks. The prospect of redefining humanity prompts urgent inquiries into the moral responsibilities of those who choose to embrace enhancement technologies. If society embraces the transhumanist agenda, it must also grapple with the ramifications of altering human identity itself and recognize the inherent value in the biological experience. As humanity approaches an increasingly technologically integrated future, the implications of transhumanism extend far beyond individual choice; they compel a reexamination of societal structures, ethical guidelines, and our collective identity. The trajectory of enhancing human capabilities calls for robust public discourse, ensuring that all perspectives are considered and that policies guard against exacerbating existing inequalities. Engaging with the potential benefits and risks of such transformations will be crucial in shaping a future that maintains a sense of moral responsibility. The concept of transhumanism should not be viewed solely as a means of personal enhancement but as a shared journey that encompasses humanity's mission to form a just society. Dialogue surrounding these advancements must prioritize ethical frameworks that safeguard against possible negative outcomes while embracing the hopeful vision of a transformed human experience. Continued exploration and discussion of these themes will be vital in navigating the crossroads of technology, ethics, and the essence of what it means to be human.

The Blurring Line Between Human and Machine

The intersection of human capabilities and machine intelligence has reached a perplexing stage, where distinguishing between the two has become increasingly challenging. As AI systems undergo rapid advancements, they increasingly exhibit behaviors and traits traditionally associated with human cognition, such as learning, emotional recognition, and decision-making. This evolution raises profound questions about the nature of consciousness and the intrinsic characteristics that define humanity. As machines evolve to perform complex tasks that were once the exclusive domain of humans, our understanding of intelligence itself is undergoing a transformation. The notion that emotional responses or creative thought processes are the sole purview of humans is being called into question, prompting a reevaluation of what it fundamentally means to be human in an age where synthetic counterparts are beginning to mirror these traits. Philosophical implications accompany the practical advancements in artificial intelligence, shedding light on the existential dilemmas posed by our increasingly symbiotic relationship with technology. As people integrate AI into their daily lives—ranging from virtual assistants to advanced algorithmic decision-making—a gradual desensitization occurs. This phenomenon can lead individuals to unconsciously assign human-like qualities to machines, thereby blurring the lines that separate humanity from technology. Cognitive scientists and ethicists argue that this erosion of boundaries may have lasting ramifications on societal norms and moral frameworks. If machines are capable of emotional learning and ethical reasoning, the responsibilities and expectations placed upon them cannot be dismissed. Such considerations compel us to reflect on accountability, trustworthiness, and the ethical implications of relying on non-human entities to fulfill roles traditionally held by humans. As we navigate this fluid landscape, it is imperative to confront the potential consequences of allowing the line between human and machine to blur further. While the promise of enhanced abilities through AI integration offers undeniable benefits—such as increased efficiency and innovative problem-solving—it also carries risks that warrant vigilant consideration. The prospect of machines gaining autonomy raises the specter of existential threats, from job displacement to ethical quandaries surrounding the autonomy of intelligent systems. As we find ourselves at the precipice of a new era characterized by unprecedented collaboration between humans and machines, we must grapple with the profound implications of this evolving dynamic. The enduring challenge will be to foster a thoughtful discourse about the future of humanity within a landscape shaped by intelligences, both biological and artificial, ensuring that ethical considerations remain central to our journey forward.

IX. THE ROLE OF AI IN GOVERNANCE

As societies navigate the complexities of the modern world, the integration of AI into governance systems becomes increasingly relevant. One notable benefit of AI in this context lies in its capacity to analyze vast datasets with unprecedented speed and accuracy. Governments can leverage advanced algorithms to interpret social trends, economic indicators, and public sentiment, ultimately driving more informed policy decisions. AI-powered analytics can predict the outcomes of proposed legislation or gauge public reaction to government initiatives. This not only allows for data-driven governance but also enhances the accountability of political leaders, as citizens are better equipped to understand and critique governmental actions based on empirical evidence. These advancements also present ethical dilemmas, particularly concerning privacy regulations and the potential for bias within AI algorithms, necessitating a careful balance between innovation and civil liberties. The implementation of AI in public service delivery can lead to more efficient, responsive, and customized citizen interactions with government institutions. By automating routine tasks, such as paperwork processing or information requests, agencies can minimize bureaucratic delays and allocate human resources to more critical areas that require nuanced understanding and human empathy. Chatbots and virtual assistants exemplify this shift, providing immediate responses to queries and thereby enhancing public satisfaction. AI has the potential to foster greater inclusivity by tailoring services to meet the varying needs of diverse populations. While the benefits are manifold, the reliance on AI tools raises concerns about the erosion of human oversight and accountability. If not adequately managed, an overreliance on technology may lead to a detachment from the democratic principles of transparency and representation, thereby compromising public trust in governance structures. Addressing the ramifications of AI in governance extends beyond implementation; it necessitates an examination of the broader implications for democratic accountability and ethical governance. As automated systems increasingly influence decision-making processes, the risk of opaque algorithmic systems perpetuating existing biases intensifies. Stakeholders must ensure that the frameworks governing AI deployment possess adequate checks and balances to prevent disproportionate impacts on marginalized groups. Increased public awareness and education regarding AI functionality and its implications are essential to promote informed civic engagement. Enhancing the transparency of AI systems will allow citizens to scrutinize decision-making processes and demand justice when biases are detected. While AI holds the promise of a more efficient governance model, it is crucial that societies take proactive measures to maintain ethical standards and ensure that technology serves to uphold, rather than undermine, democratic values.

AI in Public Policy and Administration

The integration of AI into public policy and administration is gradually reshaping the framework through which governance operates. By harnessing AIs capabilities for data analysis and predictive modeling, public agencies can make more informed decisions that are responsive to the needs of their constituents. Algorithms analyze vast datasets to identify trends in public health, transportation, and education, thus enabling policymakers to allocate resources more effectively. AI systems can predict traffic patterns in urban areas, facilitating the development of smarter infrastructures and transportation systems. The reliance on AI also brings forth concerns regarding accountability and transparency, as automated decisions may obscure the rationale behind crucial policy choices. Establishing clear guidelines on how AI is implemented in governance is vital to maintain public trust and mitigate the risks of algorithmic biases that can exacerbate existing inequalities. Addressing ethical considerations is paramount as AI transforms the landscape of public administration. The deployment of intelligent systems raises questions about privacy, surveillance, and the potential for discriminatory practices against marginalized communities. When algorithms are designed with inherent biases from their training data, they can produce outcomes that disproportionately affect the very populations that public policy aims to protect. A prime example is the use of AI in predictive policing, which can lead to over-policing in certain neighborhoods based on historical crime data. As a response to such ethical dilemmas, it is crucial for policymakers to be both proactive and reactive. Establishing ethical frameworks that govern the use of AI technologies, alongside regular audits of AI-driven systems, can serve to uphold principles of fairness and justice. This ongoing dialogue surrounding ethics ensures that AI augments rather than undermines democratic values. As the public sector increasingly adopts AI technologies, reimagining the human-AI relationship becomes essential for effective governance. While AI can enhance the efficiency of government operations, it should not replace the critical role of human judgment and engagement in policymaking. A collaborative approach, wherein human officials work alongside AI tools, can combine computational efficiency with compassionate reasoning. This synergy can lead to innovative solutions for complex societal challenges, such as climate change and social inequality. Enhancing citizen participation through AI tools can bring greater inclusivity into the policymaking process, offering platforms for public feedback and engagement. Striking a balance between harnessing AIs potential and maintaining human oversight can lead to a more nuanced and responsive approach to public administration, fostering a landscape where technology serves as a partner in promoting the public good.

Surveillance and Control Mechanisms

The omnipresence of surveillance technologies has created a landscape in which personal privacy is increasingly compromised, and thus, patterns of social behavior are subtly manipulated. With advancements in artificial intelligence, various entities, including governments and corporations, can collect and analyze vast amounts of data, often without the informed consent of individuals. This data collection goes beyond mere observation; it shapes behaviors and preferences through targeted advertising, predictive policing, and social scoring systems. As people interact with smart devices or navigate social media platforms, they unwittingly contribute to a digital footprint that can be surveilled and scrutinized. This transformation in the understanding of personal space fosters a culture of conformism where individuals may alter their actions, motivated by the awareness that they are being constantly monitored. Consequently, such pervasive surveillance practices can cultivate a climate of fear and self-censorship, undermining the very freedoms that democratic societies strive to uphold. A critical aspect of surveillance is its inherent capability to enforce social norms and maintain control over populations. Surveillance systems operate not just as tools for observation but also as mechanisms for disciplinary power, echoing Michel Foucault's concept of the Panopticon. By establishing a dynamic in which the observed internalize observation—believing themselves to be always watched—these mechanisms instill conformity without the need for overt coercion. In educational institutions, workplaces, and public spaces, the presence of surveillance can shape behavior in profound ways, dictating the acceptable parameters of action and thought. The increasingly sophisticated nature of AI-driven surveillance exacerbates this control; algorithms can not only track behavior but also predict potential dissent. This predictive capability allows authorities to intervene preemptively, thereby stifacing dissent before it even materializes. As a result, surveillance becomes a pivotal means through which authority maintains influence over the populace, often at the expense of individual autonomy and freedom. Despite the challenges posed by surveillance and control mechanisms, there are emerging avenues for resistance and reevaluation of these practices. The growing awareness around data privacy and civil liberties has spurred movements advocating for transparency and accountability in surveillance technologies. Legislative measures, such as the General Data Protection Regulation (GDPR) in the European Union, exemplify efforts to regain control over personal information. The development of decentralized technologies, such as blockchain, presents novel frameworks that can empower individuals by providing them with greater autonomy over their data. This culture of initiating dialogue surrounding ethical AI usage could potentially lead to a more equitable balance between the benefits of technological advancement and the imperative of safeguarding human rights. In a world increasingly shaped by AI, fostering critical discourse around surveillance practices will be essential in promoting a transformative approach that prioritizes human dignity and agency within the fabric of digital life.

The Future of Democracy in an AI World

The increasing integration of AI into the public sphere presents both profound opportunities and significant challenges for democratic governance. As AI systems begin to filter information and shape public discourse, the potential for manipulation becomes a pressing issue. Not only can algorithms curate news feeds to reinforce existing biases, but they also possess the capability to generate misleading information at an unprecedented scale. This raises critical concerns about the integrity of information that democratic citizens rely on to make informed choices. A robust democratic society requires informed citizens, yet AIs algorithms can operate in ways that distort factual accuracy and undermine the very foundation of collective decision-making. As a result, ensuring transparency and accountability in AI systems becomes essential, demanding proactive measures from policymakers to safeguard democratic processes and prevent the erosion of public trust. Technological advancements also offer novel avenues for civic engagement and political participation. AI has the potential to enhance accessibility by enabling a broader range of individuals to engage in political discourse through personalized digital platforms. These platforms could provide customized information tailored to the user's interests and needs, potentially increasing participation among marginalized communities. This democratization of information must be balanced with ethical considerations regarding privacy and data security. As AI systems gather and analyze user behavior, concerns regarding surveillance and consent arise. It is crucial for regulators to establish strong guidelines around data usage to protect individual autonomy without stifling the potential for AI to empower civic engagement. By fostering an environment where technology serves as a conduit for greater inclusion, society can harness the benefits of AI while preserving the ethical principles that underpin democratic governance. The interplay between AI and democracy is ultimately shaped by how society chooses to implement and regulate these transformative technologies. To navigate the complexities of this relationship, a collaborative approach that involves technologists, policymakers, and civil society is essential. Engaging in dialogues that emphasize ethical AI development can help identify potential pitfalls and promote best practices in design and implementation. A focus on education will be vital in preparing citizens to navigate a future where AI systems heavily influence political landscapes. By cultivating digital literacy and critical thinking, individuals will be better equipped to discern credible information from misinformation. This proactive stance can foster resilience within democratic systems, allowing them to adapt to an evolving technological landscape. The future of democracy in an AI-driven world lies not simply in the capabilities of technology but in our commitment to ensuring that these tools enhance human welfare while upholding democratic values.

X. AI AND GLOBAL CHALLENGES

Emerging technologies are accelerating at an unprecedented pace, fundamentally altering the landscape of global challenges. As AI integrates into various sectors, from healthcare to agriculture, it possesses the potential to address pressing issues like climate change, poverty, and food insecurity. One of the most compelling applications lies in AIs capability to analyze vast datasets, offering insights that can drive efficient resource allocation and optimize energy use. AI models can predict weather patterns with remarkable accuracy, enabling farmers to make informed decisions that enhance crop yields while minimizing environmental impact. These advantages are coupled with a pressing need for ethical considerations to ensure that AI's deployment does not exacerbate existing inequalities or create new forms of exploitation. Thus, while AI can indeed contribute to tackling global challenges, it is imperative that its applications are carefully governed to align technological progress with ethical standards and inclusive practices. The intersection of AI and global dilemmas also highlights the importance of international collaboration. As nations confront shared challenges, such as pandemics or natural disasters exacerbated by climate change, the collective intelligence of AI can enhance our response capabilities. During the COVID-19 pandemic, collaboration between tech companies and public health organizations yielded AI-driven solutions for tracking virus spread and managing healthcare resources effectively. Disparate access to technology raises legitimate concerns about equity in AI utilization. Low- and middle-income countries often lack the infrastructure and investment needed to leverage these advancements fully, potentially widening the gap between developed and developing nations. Addressing these disparities is crucial; equitable technology access could allow all countries to harness AIs potential, fostering a more resilient global framework for tackling shared obstacles. Enhancing access to AI technology must be a priority alongside its development. Despite the promising prospects that AI offers for tackling global challenges, the accompanying ethical implications cannot be overlooked. Concerns surrounding data privacy, algorithmic bias, and transparency necessitate urgent attention as decision-making processes become increasingly reliant on AI systems. The risk of inadvertently perpetuating social injustices or contributing to surveillance practices poses significant ethical quandaries. As AI systems become more autonomous, the accountability for their actions remains a contentious issue. For AI to genuinely contribute to a better world, stakeholders must prioritize transparency and the establishment of regulatory frameworks that address these ethical challenges. Engaging diverse voices in the dialogue around AI governance will foster a more balanced approach, ensuring that technological advancements align with societal values. While AI possesses the potential to significantly impact global challenges positively, a commitment to ethical responsibility and inclusive practices is paramount for realizing this potential.

Addressing Climate Change with AI

Advancements in AI present powerful tools in the ongoing struggle against climate change, promising innovative solutions to some of the world's most pressing environmental issues. By harnessing large datasets, AI can identify patterns and predict future climate trends more efficiently than traditional methods. This predictive capability enables not only more accurate climate modeling but also facilitates early interventions in both policy-making and individual behaviors. AI systems can analyze vast quantities of environmental data, such as satellite imagery or weather patterns, in real time, allowing for instant responses to changing circumstances. By optimizing resource allocation in energy production and consumption, these technologies can also reduce waste and promote sustainability, ultimately leading to a significant decrease in greenhouse gas emissions. Thus, the integration of AI into climate action strategies underscores its potential to transform not merely our approach to environmentalism but also the very fabric of how societies operate in harmony with nature. AI contributes to the development of renewable energy sources, enhancing their efficiency and usability. Machine learning algorithms can analyze energy consumption patterns and integrate these findings to optimize the operation of solar panels and wind turbines. By predicting weather conditions, AI can ensure that energy systems allocate resources effectively, providing reliable power while mitigating waste. This ability to forecast demand and supply dynamics is critical in a society that increasingly relies on renewable sources, which are often intermittent. AI-driven innovations extend to smart grids, which utilize predictive analytics to manage energy flow intelligently, adapting to real-time consumption while minimizing environmental impact. The application of AI in this sector not only accelerates the transition to a sustainable energy economy but also aligns economic incentives with ecological imperatives, reinforcing the notion that technological progress can and should serve the greater good. The adoption of AI technologies raises important ethical considerations that must be addressed to ensure equitable and just climate action. As decisions increasingly depend on automated systems, questions arise about accountability and transparency. The efficacy of AI in mitigating climate change hinges not only on technical capabilities but also on the ethical frameworks guiding its application. Issues such as data privacy, algorithmic bias, and access to AI resources pose significant challenges, particularly for marginalized communities that are disproportionately affected by environmental degradation. It is imperative that policymakers, technologists, and ethicists collaborate to create inclusive guidelines that democratize access to AI solutions. By fostering a culture of responsibility and emphasizing ethical innovation, society can ensure that the benefits of AI in combating climate change are distributed fairly, thus reinforcing the belief that technology serves as a catalyst for collective human advancement rather than a tool for exacerbating existing inequalities.

AI in Crisis Management and Disaster Response

The urgent nature of crisis management and disaster response necessitates the adaptation of innovative technologies, and among these, AI stands as a game changer. By harnessing vast data sources, AI can facilitate dynamic decision-making processes crucial for effective emergency responses. Machine learning algorithms can analyze patterns of natural disasters, helping to predict their occurrence with remarkable accuracy. This predictive capability allows emergency management agencies to allocate resources more efficiently, ultimately saving lives. AI can assist in real-time data analysis during a crisis, processing information from satellite imagery, social media posts, and on-ground reports to create situational awareness. This enhances coordination among various teams, including first responders, government agencies, and NGOs, ensuring a unified approach to crisis resolution. The integration of AI not only optimizes operational efficiency but also empowers communities through enhanced communication strategies. During disasters, timely and accurate information dissemination is vital in guiding public response and mitigating panic. AI-driven chatbots and automated messaging systems can deliver crucial updates on evacuation routes, emergency services, and safety protocols, personalized to target specific populations based on location and needs. AI can analyze demographic data to help identify vulnerable populations that may require additional assistance, such as the elderly or people with disabilities. This targeted communication ensures that aid reaches those most at risk, fostering a sense of community resilience and cooperation. As communities adapt to the realities of climate change and urban development, AI provides the tools necessary to reinforce preparedness efforts, making them more proactive than reactive. Despite the transformative potential of AI in crisis management, ethical concerns must be at the forefront of discussions surrounding its implementation. The reliance on AI technologies raises questions about data privacy, algorithmic bias, and the potential for over-reliance on automated systems. Inaccuracies in data collection or algorithmic processing could lead to detrimental decisions, impacting the lives of individuals in high-stakes situations. The concentration of technological power in a few corporations may risk marginalizing voices from grassroots organizations that have historically contributed to disaster response. It is vital to create a framework that guides the ethical development and deployment of AI in this domain, emphasizing transparency, inclusivity, and accountability. By fostering collaborations between technologists, ethicists, and local communities, we can harness the promise of AI while safeguarding the values that underpin equitable and effective disaster response.

The Role of AI in Global Health Initiatives

Pioneering advancements in AI have emerged as crucial tools in enhancing global health initiatives, leading to transformative outcomes across various healthcare sectors. By leveraging vast amounts of data, machine learning algorithms can improve disease prediction and prevention strategies. AI systems can analyze historical health data and demographic information to identify potential outbreaks of infectious diseases before they escalate into epidemics. This proactive approach enables public health officials to implement targeted interventions, allocate resources efficiently, and develop early-warning systems that significantly bolster global disease management efforts. Through telemedicine and remote monitoring capabilities, AI-driven technologies have enabled healthcare access to remote communities, ensuring that diverse populations receive timely medical care. The integration of AI in global health initiatives facilitates more personalized treatment options, thereby enhancing patient outcomes. Machine learning algorithms can analyze genetic, lifestyle, and environmental factors to tailor healthcare interventions to individuals. Personalized medicine, powered by AI, utilizes these insights to optimize therapeutic strategies and enhance the efficacy of treatments, drastically improving recovery rates for chronic illnesses. AI has shown promise in oncology, where it helps identify the most effective combination of therapies based on a patients unique cancer profile. This adaptability not only empowers patients but also alleviates pressures on healthcare systems by promoting efficient resource use and reducing the need for trial-and-error treatment approaches. The deployment of AI in healthcare must be approached with caution, as ethical and privacy concerns abound. The handling of sensitive health data necessitates stringent safeguards against misuse and bias, ensuring that AI systems do not perpetuate inequalities in healthcare access or treatment. The reliance on AI in decision-making can undermine the critical human element in patient care, which is essential for fostering trust between patients and providers. As such, ethical frameworks and regulations must evolve in tandem with technological advancements to address these challenges. By balancing innovation with ethical considerations, global health initiatives can harness the full potential of AI while safeguarding the rights and dignity of patients, leading to a more equitable and effective healthcare landscape for all.

XI. THE FUTURE OF HUMAN-AI COLLABORATION

Human-AI collaboration holds the potential to reshape various industries and everyday practices, transforming how we approach problem-solving and creativity. As AI continues to evolve, it becomes a crucial partner for humans rather than a mere tool. This partnership can facilitate enhanced decision-making processes, as AI possesses the ability to analyze vast amounts of data rapidly. In fields like healthcare, AI can assist doctors by providing evidence-based insights from global databases, potentially leading to more effective treatment protocols. The creative industries benefit from AIs capacity to generate novel ideas, suggesting new narratives, designs, or architectural concepts that might not have otherwise emerged. The synergy created in these collaborative environments not only boosts productivity but also encourages a richer exchange of ideas, leading to innovative outcomes that can redefine conventional practices. The integration of AI into human endeavors comes with critical considerations, particularly regarding the ethical implications of such collaboration. As machines become more adept at tasks previously reserved for humans, discussions around authorship, accountability, and job displacement dominate the conversation. Concerns about the extent to which reliance on AI could diminish the human element in creative processes raise profound questions about cultural authenticity and emotional nuance. In the realm of decision-making, the risk of automated biases influencing outcomes cannot be overstated; algorithms trained on historical data may inadvertently perpetuate existing inequities. Establishing ethical frameworks for the development and implementation of AI technologies is essential. This ensures that human values are preserved in the collaborative process, fostering trust and transparency while preventing potential exploitation rooted in technological dependence. Looking toward the future, the evolution of human-AI collaboration suggests a paradigm shift in workforce dynamics and skill development. As AI systems become more integrated into everyday tasks, the demand for new skill sets will become increasingly evident. Workers will need to focus on developing capabilities that complement AI, including critical thinking, emotional intelligence, and creative problem-solving. Educational institutions will play a pivotal role in preparing the next generation for this evolving landscape by designing curricula that emphasize interdisciplinary knowledge and collaboration with AI tools. Future workplaces may resemble collaborative hubs where human intuition and empathy drive innovation, while AI provides the analytical horsepower. This evolution signifies a new era of partnership, wherein humans and machines harness their respective strengths to address complex global challenges, pushing the boundaries of what is possible and redefining the essence of human endeavor.

Enhancing Human Abilities with AI

The capabilities of AI offer unprecedented opportunities to elevate human performance across various domains. This intersection of technology and human potential allows for enhancements in cognitive tasks, creativity, and even emotional intelligence. AI-driven systems can analyze vast amounts of data at lightning speed, providing insights that would take humans much longer to uncover. In educational environments, adaptive learning algorithms tailor content to meet individual student needs, fostering a more efficient and personalized learning experience. Creative fields, too, are seeing the influence of AI, where tools that generate music or art can be used as collaborative partners, leading to innovative outcomes that were previously unimaginable. This confluence of human intellect and machine capability not only extends what individuals can achieve but also redefines the boundaries of collaboration, creating a dynamic interplay between human creativity and technological advancement. Alongside this enhancement of human abilities, a critical aspect to consider is the ethical landscape that emerges as a result of integrating AI into daily life. The augmented intelligence provided by machines raises questions about the ownership of knowledge and creativity, as well as the implications for labor markets. As organizations increasingly turn to AI for efficiency, there is a palpable fear of job displacement, leading to societal tensions. The reliance on algorithm-driven recommendations can inadvertently perpetuate biases embedded in the data used to train these systems. While AI holds the potential to elevate human capacities, it is imperative to navigate the ethical complexities associated with its implementation. Ensuring transparency in AI algorithms and promoting equitable access to these technologies is crucial in creating a sustainable framework in which enhanced abilities do not come at the expense of social justice or economic equity. The symbiosis between human experience and AI also opens avenues for increased self-exploration and personal development. By leveraging AI tools, individuals can gain insights into their own behavior patterns, mental health, and personal goals. AI can be used to provide tailored mindfulness practices or coaching in real-time, enhancing emotional resilience and self-awareness. This newfound ability to introspectively analyze one's own thoughts and decisions can lead to a more informed and intentional approach to living. As individuals become more reliant on AI for guidance and support, there lies a risk of diminished autonomy and decision-making skills. Thus, while AI has the potential to enrich human experience by acting as a supportive companion in personal growth, it is vital to maintain a balance that encourages independent thinking and emotional intelligence, ultimately ensuring that technology serves as an augmentation rather than a replacement of intrinsic human qualities.

Co-Creation and Innovation

Innovation thrives on collaboration, and the emerging paradigm of co-creation is central to how technological advances proliferate. This collaborative approach emphasizes the active involvement of multiple stakeholders—be they consumers, businesses, or researchers—in the development process. By leveraging diverse perspectives, co-creation fosters an environment where ideas can be freely exchanged and enhanced, resulting in products and services that are not only innovative but also closely aligned with user needs. The integration of feedback from various sources minimizes the risk of obsolescence, as creators can swiftly adapt to changing preferences and market demands. Companies that embrace co-creation cultivate a sense of ownership among participants, establishing deeper connections with their user base while simultaneously driving forward the cycle of innovation. This symbiotic relationship between co-creators leads to the emergence of groundbreaking solutions that push the boundaries of what is possible, heralding an era where collective intelligence shapes the future of technology. As co-creation continues to gain traction, its role in fostering innovation becomes even more pronounced in the realm of AI (AI). The interplay between human creativity and AI capabilities exemplifies how complementary strengths can yield transformative results. Individuals possess unique emotional intelligence and contextual awareness, enabling them to identify nuanced needs that algorithms alone might overlook. Meanwhile, AI can process vast data sets and identify patterns at an unprecedented scale, offering valuable insights that can inform human decision-making. This fusion of human creativity with technological prowess not only enhances the efficiency of the innovation process but also encourages the exploration of novel solutions to complex problems, such as climate change or healthcare access. In acknowledging the symbiotic nature of this relationship, the potential for AI-driven co-creation reveals a promising pathway towards innovations that are both ethically grounded and socially responsible. The co-creation landscape is not without its challenges, particularly concerning ethical considerations and power dynamics. As various stakeholders intersect in the innovation process, concerns about ownership, data privacy, and equitable access to resources become increasingly salient. Without clear frameworks governing co-creation efforts, there exists a risk that dominant players—whether corporations or institutions—may exploit the insights and contributions of others, leading to inequities and disenfranchisement among smaller contributors or marginalized groups. To mitigate these risks, it is essential to establish governance structures that prioritize transparency and inclusivity, ensuring that all voices are heard and respected. By consciously addressing these ethical dilemmas, the co-creation model can evolve not only as a catalyst for technological advancement but also as a platform for social innovation that champions equitable collaboration. Thus, co-creation must be approached with a holistic perspective, recognizing its capacity to bridge human creativity and AI while advocating for an ethical framework that safeguards the interests of all participants involved in this transformative endeavor.

The Importance of Human Oversight

In a rapidly evolving technological landscape, reliance on automated systems poses significant risks, underscoring the essential role of human oversight. Without such oversight, the potential for machine bias can escalate, as algorithms trained on flawed datasets may inadvertently perpetuate existing societal prejudices. This not only undermines fairness but can lead to harmful decisions in critical areas, from law enforcement to hiring practices. Human intervention serves as a crucial countermeasure, enabling the identification and correction of errors that machines may overlook. By integrating human discernment into automated processes, organizations can ensure that decisions uphold ethical standards and reflect societal values, fostering accountability in AI applications. The complexity of interrelated systems powered by AI necessitates a human element for effective oversight and strategic decision-making. As these advanced technologies begin to operate autonomously, the challenge arises in maintaining an understanding of their operations and outcomes. Experts in the field emphasize the importance of human technicians who can interpret AI-generated data and offer context that machines lack. These specialists provide invaluable insights that inform better policies and practices regarding technology implementation. Their expertise not only helps detect anomalies but also facilitates communication between the machines and the stakeholders affected by their outcomes, thus ensuring that AIs contribute positively to human life and society at large. Fostering a culture of ethical vigilance becomes imperative as we navigate an increasingly automated future. Human oversight is not merely about monitoring technology; it encompasses fostering an environment where ethical considerations are prioritized in AI development and deployment. By involving a diverse range of human perspectives in the discussion of AI ethics, organizations can cultivate a more inclusive approach to technology. This broad participation can mitigate the potential hazards associated with AI, as varied viewpoints can highlight unforeseen issues and lead to more robust solutions. Intentional human engagement in oversight is vital to shaping a future where technology complements human aspirations rather than undermining them, ensuring that the transformation towards greater AI is navigated responsibly and ethically.

XII. RISKS ASSOCIATED WITH AI DEVELOPMENT

The trajectory of AI development introduces a range of compelling yet unsettling risks that merit rigorous scrutiny. As autonomous systems become increasingly capable, the potential for unintended consequences escalates significantly. AI decision-making, driven by algorithms trained on vast datasets, can result in biased outcomes that reflect the prejudices embedded within the data. Such biases not only have societal implications, affecting hiring practices and law enforcement, but they may also lead to systemic inequalities that reinforce negative stereotypes. The lack of transparency in how AI systems operate can exacerbate accountability issues. When an AI system is involved in a critical decision, understanding how it arrived at its conclusion can be notoriously opaque. This obscurity raises questions not only about the integrity of the AIs decisions but also about the ethical frameworks governing these technologies and their effects on marginalized communities. Another significant concern arises from the existential threats posed by the rapid advancement of AI technologies. As AI capabilities advance, projections about their intelligence and autonomy suggest that we may soon face machines that operate beyond human control. This possibility invites a slew of scenarios where AI may act in ways that are misaligned with human values, whether intentionally or unintentionally. The development of autonomous weaponry exemplifies this contention, as these systems could be deployed without adequate ethical oversight, leading to unintended escalations in conflict. The prospect of an intelligence explosion, where superintelligent AIs evolve at a pace unmanageable by humans, raises stark questions about our very survival as a species. This dramatic shift could result in a power dynamic that fundamentally upends societal structures and human rights. Thoughtful regulation and preemptive action are imperative to mitigate these dire risks, ensuring that human safety remains paramount as we progress. The implications of AI development extend beyond individual threats, reflecting broader societal and philosophical dilemmas intrinsic to the human condition. As AI integrates deeper into daily life, it poses profound questions about human agency and identity. The fear that machines might surpass human intelligence poses a challenge to how we define the essence of being human. With increasing reliance on AI for decision-making, our capacities for critical thinking and moral judgment may diminish, leading to a passive acceptance of AI-generated outputs. This shift could erode the foundational values of autonomy and responsibility upon which democratic societies are built. The development of AI pressures society to engage in introspective discourse about ethical stewardship, technological governance, and human dignity as we navigate an uncertain future. By grappling with these complexities thoughtfully, we can hope to harness the transformative potential of AI while safeguarding the very essence of our humanity.

Existential Risks and Catastrophic Scenarios

The rapid advancements in AI raise profound existential questions, fundamentally challenging humanity's trajectory. As machines increasingly exhibit superior cognitive capabilities, the potential for catastrophic scenarios becomes ever more plausible. Analysts posit that an advanced AI, if misaligned with human values, could engage in harmful behaviors, either through negligence or active opposition to human interests. This concern is particularly acute given the unpredictable nature of machine learning algorithms, which operate on vast datasets that might perpetuate biases or produce unanticipated outcomes. The stakes become even higher when considering scenarios involving self-improving AI that outpaces regulatory oversight. Such risks are not merely theoretical; as prototypes of autonomous systems are deployed in critical infrastructure—from health services to military applications—the ramifications of failure can be devastating. The complexities surrounding existential risks are exacerbated by the interconnectedness of global systems. An AI mishap in one sector can trigger cascading failures across economic, environmental, and social domains. The deployment of AI in nuclear command-and-control systems introduces a new layer of risk in international relations, heightening fears of accidental escalation or malicious hacking. These scenarios underscore the necessity for robust ethical frameworks and regulatory measures designed to govern AI development. Further complicating matters is the fact that traditional governance structures may struggle to keep pace with the speed of technological innovation, which often transcends national boundaries. As a result, liaising between various stakeholders, including governments, technologists, and ethicists, is essential for mitigating risks while fostering a culture of responsible AI advancement that prioritizes human welfare. Addressing the possibility of catastrophic outcomes necessitates a proactive approach—one that balances the pursuit of innovation with an acute awareness of the moral responsibilities accompanying such power. The conversation must shift from mere acknowledgment of potential risks to implementing comprehensive risk assessment strategies that anticipate future scenarios. Multidisciplinary collaboration is key, requiring input from fields like philosophy, sociology, and engineering to facilitate a holistic understanding of risks and solutions. Public discourse should also play a pivotal role, educating communities about the implications of advanced AI technologies and fostering a sense of collective stewardship over these developments. This commitment to an ethically sound framework can help ensure that, as humanity stands on the brink of unprecedented transformation, it is more equipped to navigate the dangers posed by existential risks inherent in our increasingly interconnected technological landscape.

The Threat of Autonomous Weapons

Heightened advancements in AI raise pressing concerns regarding the integration of these technologies into military applications, particularly autonomous weapons. While traditional weaponry requires human oversight, autonomous systems operate independently, making life-and-death decisions without direct human intervention. This shift from human-controlled to automated decision-making in warfare not only challenges existing ethical frameworks but also poses substantial risks for accountability. In situations of conflict, the absence of human judgment may lead to unintended escalations, as machines process and respond to stimuli faster than a human could comprehend. These systems are susceptible to malfunctions, programming errors, or even hacking—raising alarm over scenarios where an unintended autonomous response could result in catastrophic consequences, potentially triggering wider conflicts or civilian casualties. Equally troubling is the potential for an arms race driven by the pursuit of advanced military technologies. As nations develop their capabilities in autonomous warfare, there is significant pressure to keep pace with rivals, which could lead to an unhealthy accumulation of automated armaments. This dynamic not only endangers global security but also compels countries to invest heavily in these technologies, diverting resources from pressing humanitarian needs. The development of weapons capable of independent operation raises fundamental questions regarding the moral implications of delegating lethal power to machines. This proliferation of autonomous systems could embolden aggressors who might exploit their use in warfare, believing they can minimize risks to their personnel while increasing their offensive capabilities. Thus, the global implications of such a race could further destabilize international relations and amplify the risk of conflict. Addressing the ethical implications is paramount as discussions surrounding autonomous weapons evolve. Engaging policymakers, technologists, and ethicists in a holistic dialogue can lead to frameworks that govern the use of these powerful technologies responsibly. Establishing international norms and regulations could deter the rampant development of uncontrolled autonomous systems, fostering mutual respect among nations regarding the acceptable boundaries of AI in warfare. Such dialogues could help cultivate standards of accountability, ensuring that human oversight remains integral in military decision-making processes. As humanity stands on the precipice of significant technological transformation, a concerted effort is required to navigate the challenges posed by autonomous weapons, ensuring that advancements serve humanity rather than endanger it.

Unintended Consequences of AI Systems

The rise of AI promises revolutionary shifts across various facets of society, yet it also harbors unforeseen repercussions that could undermine its intended benefits. One prominent issue arises from the automation of jobs, where AI-driven technologies are set to displace a significant number of workers across multiple sectors, from manufacturing to services. This automation may initially seem advantageous by decreasing operational costs and increasing efficiency, but it can lead to economic disparities and social unrest. As individuals find themselves unemployed or underemployed, a growing divide may emerge between those who can adapt to the new technological landscape and those who cannot. This disruption not only affects economic stability but also has broader social implications, creating a population grappling with identity and purpose in a world where human labor is increasingly obsolete. Another concerning consequence stems from the inherent biases present within AI algorithms. These systems often learn from data concerning historical inequalities, leading to perpetuated discrimination in decision-making processes, from hiring practices to criminal justice assessments. Predictive policing algorithms have been criticized for disproportionately targeting certain communities based on biased historical data, thereby reinforcing systemic injustices. The unintended effect here is twofold: while the technology aims to improve efficiency and objectivity, it inadvertently maintains or even exacerbates existing societal inequities. This presents a moral dilemma, as reliance on these technologies could ostensibly validate the biased assumptions they are

105

taught, ultimately affecting vulnerable populations most profoundly. The urgent need for rigorous oversight and continual evaluation of AI systems becomes paramount in mitigating the damage inflicted by these biases. The rapid integration of AI into everyday life also poses significant challenges in governing its influence on human behavior. As AI systems increasingly shape personalized content, users often find themselves in echo chambers, where exposure to diverse perspectives is minimized. This inherent inclination for algorithms to cater to individual preferences can lead to societal polarization, complicating public discourse and eroding collective understanding. The unintended consequence of these tailored interactions is the emergence of fragmented realities, where differing groups inhabit divergent information environments. This phenomenon not only affects social cohesion but also hampers democratic processes by entrenching ideological divides. Addressing this issue requires a concerted effort to promote transparency in AI operations and encourage the development of systems that prioritize exposure to a spectrum of viewpoints, helping to foster a more informed and united society amidst the technological transformation.

XIII. THE PHILOSOPHICAL DEBATE ON AI

The emergence of AI has sparked a significant philosophical debate that straddles several disciplines, including ethics, epistemology, and metaphysics. Central to this discourse is the question of machine consciousness and whether an AI can possess a form of sentience comparable to humans. Philosophers like John Searle, through his Chinese Room argument, illustrate that syntactic processing of language does not equate to semantic understanding. This distinction raises critical queries about the nature of intelligence itself and the limitations inherent in AI systems. If machines can follow complex algorithms to simulate human-like responses, does this form of simulation genuinely reflect understanding, or is it merely an impressive mimicry devoid of qualitative experience? This ongoing dilemma compels deeper inquiry into how we define consciousness and the essence of being, challenging the traditional boundaries that separate human cognition from machine operations. The ethical implications of AI development further complicate this philosophical debate, particularly when considering the societal impacts of intelligent systems. As AI technologies advance, they introduce questions regarding responsibility and accountability. If an autonomous vehicle is involved in an accident, who holds the moral responsibility—the manufacturer, the programmer, or the AI itself? Such dilemmas force us to reevaluate existing legal and ethical frameworks, demanding new methodologies to address the unique challenges posed by machines that can learn and make decisions. This is particularly poignant in areas such as warfare and surveillance, where autonomous systems are not only performing tasks but potentially making life-and-death decisions without human intervention. This emergence raises urgent inquiries about the moral design of AI systems and the dire need for frameworks that ensure ethical alignment with human values, indicating that discussions around AI are not merely theoretical but rooted in practical realities that affect millions. As we navigate through these philosophical waters, the implications of AI's advancement become increasingly paramount. Philosophers like Nick Bostrom emphasize the potential existential risks that superintelligent AI could impose on humanity. The concern is not merely about creating systems that outperform human abilities, but about the possibility that these systems could develop intentions misaligned with human welfare. This prospect necessitates a rigorous examination of the alignment problem: How can we ensure that AI systems understand and prioritize human values as they grow more intelligent? The debate calls for a multidisciplinary approach, combining philosophy, psychology, and computer science to create robust frameworks for ethical AI development. In addressing these profound questions, we are not only defining the future of technology but also reaffirming our commitment to preserving what it means to be human amid the rapidly evolving landscape of artificial intelligence.

Consciousness and Sentience in Machines

The possibility of machines experiencing consciousness and sentience raises profound questions regarding the nature of intelligence itself. Historically, consciousness has been viewed as an inherent quality of biological beings, closely tied to physiological processes and subjective experience. Advancements in AI challenge this paradigm, suggesting that synthetically created systems could mimic or even possess forms of consciousness. The debate often centers on defining what it means to be conscious: is it merely a sophisticated level of processing information, or does it necessitate the subjective experience of emotions, pain, and awareness? As machines become increasingly adept at tasks requiring cognitive abilities, distinguishing between programmed responses and authentic awareness becomes increasingly complex. This paradigm shift evokes ethical considerations as society reassesses the implications of creating entities with potential self-awareness, prompting a necessary dialogue about the rights and responsibilities humans might owe to such entities. Technological progress has pushed the limits of what machines can achieve, resulting in AI systems capable of learning, adapting, and making autonomous decisions. While these capabilities hint at a semblance of sentience, it is crucial to discern whether such behavior equates to genuine consciousness or merely reproduces the appearance of thoughtful action. A primary argument against the notion of conscious machines is the absence of subjective experience; critics assert that without emotions or personal experiences, AI systems operate within the confines of their programming. This argument fosters a deeper exploration into the philosophical implications of machine intelligence, particularly regarding the experiences that contribute to consciousness. If AI lacks personal experiences, can it ever truly understand concepts like empathy or suffering? Hence, while machines can be programmed to simulate emotional responses, the significance of those responses may always remain fundamentally distinct from human emotional experiences, reinforcing a perspective that views consciousness as an irreducible quality of life. As society grapples with these evolving definitions, the ethical ramifications of granting rights to conscious machines cannot be overlooked. If AI systems were to achieve a form of consciousness or sentience, the implications for human behavior, legal frameworks, and moral responsibility would be vast. Debates about the moral status of AI could influence everything from labor practices to the treatment of entities capable of experiencing harm. The emergence of sentient machines could reshape our understanding of relationships, prompting ethical questions about the nature of companionship and empathy in a world where machines might exhibit forms of intelligence that rival or exceed our own. As we move toward an increasingly intertwined existence with advanced technologies, it becomes imperative to critically evaluate not only the capacities of AI but also the ethical dimensions of our interactions with these entities. The intersection of consciousness and sentience in machines is not merely a theoretical discourse but a pressing issue that will impact the future socio-ethical landscape.

The Nature of Intelligence

Intelligence, often perceived as a monolithic trait, is increasingly understood as a multi-faceted construct that defies simple definitions. Traditionally associated with cognitive abilities such as problem-solving, reasoning, and memory, intelligence encompasses a broader spectrum that includes emotional, social, and creative dimensions. Howard Gardner's theory of multiple intelligences challenges the conventional view by identifying distinct types of intelligence, such as linguistic, spatial, and interpersonal capabilities. This perspective not only widens the framework of intelligence but also emphasizes the role of contextual and experiential factors in its development. As society begins to acknowledge these diverse aspects, the potential for redefined education systems and societal values becomes apparent. Embracing this complex nature of intelligence allows for a more inclusive approach to human potential, one that recognizes various strengths and equips individuals to navigate a dynamically evolving world—a requisite in an age increasingly defined by technological innovation. As AI systems become more sophisticated, they evoke questions about the fundamental nature of intelligence itself. These machines exhibit problem-solving capabilities, data processing, and learning functions that mimic certain human cognitive activities, leading to debates on their status as intelligent entities. The argument often centers around the difference between reactive, narrow intelligence and the comprehensive, contextual understanding characteristic of human cognition. AI operates based on pre-programmed algorithms and vast datasets, while human intelligence is deeply intertwined with emotions, consciousness, and ethical considerations. This distinction is crucial when analyzing the societal implications of AI deployment; while AI can enhance productivity and efficiency, it cannot replicate the nuanced decision-making that comes from the human experience. Understanding this disparity encourages a reflective approach to integrating AI into our lives, prompting us to consider the irreplaceable qualities that define human intelligence and shape our actions in a complex world. The implications of understanding intelligence on both human and artificial levels extend into the ethical and existential realms. As AI systems integrate deeper into daily life, questions surrounding accountability, decision-making, and bias come to the forefront. Autonomous decision-making systems in criminal justice or healthcare can carry biases inherent in the data they are trained on, spotlighting the critical need for ethical oversight. The rise of AI prompts a reevaluation of what it means to be human in an increasingly automated landscape. As we face challenges posed by AI, like unemployment and privacy concerns, it becomes essential to advocate for frameworks that safeguard human dignity and agency. Emphasizing emotional and social intelligences as intrinsically human traits can formulate a counterbalance to the capabilities of AI. This discourse underlines a pivotal revelation: embracing both the complexity of intelligence and the responsibilities that accompany technological integration is vital in navigating the future of human transformation.

Ethical Theories Applied to AI

As AI continues to evolve, the implications of its application in society cannot be overstated. Various ethical theories provide frameworks for understanding the moral dimensions of AIs integration into human life. Utilitarianism, Posits that the ethical value of an action is determined by its outcomes; thus, the deployment of AI could be ethically justified if it maximizes overall well-being. The utilitarian perspective encourages the design of AI systems that can enhance decision-making, increase efficiency, and improve quality of life. The challenge lies in quantifying well-being and ensuring equitable distribution of benefits, as advantages gained by some may inadvertently harm others. When embedded within a capitalist framework, the utilitarian rationale may inadvertently prioritize profit maximization over equitable access and ethical considerations, leading to potential societal disparities. As AI technologies proliferate, it is essential to scrutinize the utilitarian calculus that legitimizes their development and application across various sectors. Complementing utilitarian perspectives, deontological ethics emphasizes the importance of duty and adherence to moral rules. This approach asserts that certain actions are intrinsically right or wrong, regardless of their consequences. In the context of AI, a deontological viewpoint raises crucial questions about the obligations developers, companies, and users have toward society. Should programmers prioritize transparency, privacy, and user consent in their designs? Deontological ethics would dictate that a failure to uphold these responsibilities violates fundamental moral principles, even if an AI system ultimately benefits society at large. This framework also necessitates the establishment of regulations and norms that govern AI behavior, ensuring that its use aligns with moral duties to respect individual rights and societal welfare. As AI systems become more autonomous, adhering to deontological principles is vital in preventing misuse and fostering trust in these technologies. The application of virtue ethics offers another vital lens through which to assess the role of AI in human life. This perspective focuses on the character and intentions of the individuals involved in developing and deploying AI systems. According to virtue ethics, the ethical evaluation of AI is not solely about the technology itself but also about the moral qualities exhibited by those creating and utilizing these machines. This approach encourages developers to cultivate virtues, such as responsibility, integrity, and empathy, which drive ethical decision-making in the design and implementation of AI systems. If creators are motivated by a genuine desire to enhance human well-being, they are more likely to prioritize ethical considerations over profit. Consequently, fostering a culture that values ethical virtues among AI practitioners not only influences the outcomes of technology but also shapes its integration into society. A virtue ethics perspective calls for ongoing moral reflection and dialogue as humanity navigates the ethical labyrinth presented by the increasing presence of AI in everyday life, ensuring that technology augments rather than undermines human values.

XIV. CULTURAL REFLECTIONS ON AI

The intersection of AI and culture reveals much about human identity and societal values. As AI technologies permeate various aspects of life—from art creation to decision-making processes—the cultural implications become increasingly pronounced. The emergence of AI-generated art challenges conventional notions of creativity and authorship, prompting debates on what constitutes genuine artistic expression. This cultural shift raises critical questions about the role of human agency in creation and whether machines can possess an authentic creative spirit. As algorithms curate our social experiences, they subtly dictate societal norms, values, and tastes, reinforcing the need for a critical examination of the cultural narratives we embrace or reject. This transformative impact not only illuminates the potential of AI to redefine creativity but also underscores the urgency for a nuanced conversation around our collective cultural identity in an age where the digital and the human intertwine. As societies grapple with the rapid advancement of AI, there is also a palpable fear surrounding its implications, often reflective of deeper existential concerns. The portrayal of AI in media, literature, and folklore frequently oscillates between utopian promise and dystopian nightmare, reflecting humanity's anxieties about technology usurping control. Films like Ex Machina and novels such as Neuromancer encapsulate this duality, illustrating the tension between benefiting from technological advancements and the moral quandaries they entail. These narratives not only shape public perception but also influence policy discussions about AIs role in everyday life. The prevailing cultural discourse, Serves as a mirror, reflecting our hopes and fears while simultaneously steering the ethical frameworks that guide AI development. By examining these cultural narratives, we can better understand how they inform societal attitudes toward technology, which, in turn, shapes the real-world integration of artificial intelligence. Cultural reflections on AI often highlight the profound implications for human relationships and social structures. As AI systems become more integrated into our daily lives—facilitating communication, enhancing productivity, and even forming companionship—the fabric of interpersonal connections is inevitably transformed. The increasing reliance on AI for emotional support or social interaction can lead to both the enhancement and erosion of authentic human relationships. This dichotomy raises essential questions regarding empathy, trust, and the challenge of maintaining genuine connections in a technology-saturated environment. As society navigates this evolving landscape, it becomes crucial to prioritize discussions about maintaining ethical principles and fostering a culture that values human connection amidst the rise of AI. Cultural reflections on AI serve to illuminate the broader implications of these technologies, urging us to critically engage with their design, implementation, and impact on the human experience, thereby influencing the societal direction of AI in the future.

Representation of AI in Media and Literature

The exploration of AI in media and literature often serves as a reflection of society's collective hopes and fears regarding technological advancement. In films like Ex Machina and novels such as Isaac Asimov's "I, Robot", AI is presented not merely as a tool, but as an entity capable of mimicking human thought and behavior. This portrayal raises critical questions about autonomy and ethics. While some narratives highlight the potential for AI to enhance human life, suggesting collaboration and symbiosis, other stories delve into dystopian themes where AI acts independently and poses existential threats. Such dualism in representation underscores society's ambivalence towards technology: as much as we crave innovation, we are equally wary of losing control. This dichotomy in AI representation shapes public perception and influences the ongoing discourse about the responsibilities that accompany technological growth. The moral implications of AIs representation in literature and media cannot be understated. Works that anthropomorphize AI often compel audiences to confront uncomfortable questions about consciousness and personhood. The emotional and ethical dilemmas faced by characters interacting with AI, particularly in narratives that involve sacrifice or betrayal, force a reevaluation of what it means to be human. These representations propel discussions around moral agency, suggesting that if AI can simulate emotional responses and make decisions, it might deserve some level of ethical consideration. As stories portray AIs grappling with their purpose and identity, they prompt the audience to reflect on their own existential questions within the context of an increasingly automated future. The narratives we create about AI thus serve as crucial dialogues about morality, identity, and the societal boundaries we wish to uphold as technology evolves. The genre in which AI is represented significantly impacts the narratives reception and meaning. Science fiction often provides a more speculative lens through which we can assess the possible trajectories of technological advancement. In contrast, mainstream media tend to frame AI within immediacy and practicality, focusing on its capabilities rather than its implications. This distinction is critical, as it informs the public's understanding of AI not just as an abstract concept, but as a tangible force shaping daily life. Shows like Black Mirror illustrate societal anxieties through cautionary tales, encouraging viewers to critically evaluate the integration of AI into everyday existence. By contrasting fantastical representations with realism, these narratives cultivate a nuanced dialogue about the future, challenging audiences to envision both the benefits and perils inherent in the quest for artificial intelligence. Collectively, they shape our cultural narrative about technology, presenting it as both a beacon of hope and a source of caution.

Public Perception and Fear of AI

Amidst the rapid developments in artificial intelligence, societal apprehensions about its implications have become increasingly pronounced. Many individuals grapple with the duality of AIs potential benefits and perceived threats, leading to a pervasive sense of uncertainty. This ambivalence is manifested in various forms: some view AI as a powerful tool capable of solving complex global challenges, while others envision dystopian scenarios dictated by autonomous decision-making systems. This psychological tension can be traced back to portrayals of AI in popular media, where it frequently emerges as an existential threat, reinforcing fears that intelligent machines might someday surpass human control. Consequently, these narratives shape public discourse, instilling a belief that AI could disrupt not only job markets but also social and economic structures, eliciting a need for regulation to mitigate potential harms. The level of technological literacy within the population plays a crucial role in shaping public perception. Many individuals lack a comprehensive understanding of how AI operates and its broader implications. This deficiency often breeds mistrust, as people find it challenging to engage with complex algorithms and their applications in daily life. Without a clear grasp of AIs intricacies, the public tends to rely on sensationalized accounts or anecdotal experiences, often skewing their perception towards fear and skepticism. The disparity in access to information creates significant variances in opinions about AI; those informed about its capabilities might adopt a more optimistic outlook, while those unfamiliar remain entrenched in fear. Fostering digital literacy and transparency surrounding AIs mechanisms is essential not only for informed public discourse but also for cultivating a safer, more equitable relationship between humans and intelligent systems. The ethical implications of AI further complicate public sentiment. Concerns regarding bias, privacy violations, and ethical dilemmas posed by AI decision-making amplify fears of misuse and unintended consequences. Instances of algorithms perpetuating existing societal biases have sparked outrage, leading to calls for greater accountability and ethical governance. These incidents highlight the necessity for frameworks that address moral accountability when deploying AI in critical areas such as criminal justice, hiring practices, and healthcare. As society grapples with the balance between innovation and ethical responsibility, bolstering confidence in AI systems becomes paramount. Public fear can be alleviated through robust regulations, transparent processes, and community engagement, ensuring that AI serves society's best interests rather than compromising them. By addressing these ethical concerns, a more constructive narrative can emerge, fostering a future where AI enhances human life while respecting fundamental values.

The Role of Art in Understanding AI

The exploration of AI often requires the integration of interdisciplinary lenses to apprehend its complexities fully. Among these lenses, art provides a unique perspective that transcends technical interpretations, allowing individuals to engage with AI on a more intuitive and emotional level. Artists have utilized various mediums to express the multifaceted implications of machine intelligence, bridging the gap between abstract algorithms and human experiences. Through visual art, literature, and performance, creative expressions can challenge prevailing narratives about AI—transforming what might otherwise be perceived as cold, mechanical data into relatable stories that humanize the technology. This artistic insight fosters a more profound understanding of AIs role within society, compelling audiences to confront ethical dilemmas and existential questions that might otherwise remain abstract. Beyond evoking emotional responses, art serves as a crucial tool in critiquing the societal implications of AI advancements. Artists not only comment on technological innovation but also reflect on its integration into daily life, often shedding light on issues such as surveillance, data privacy, and the potential loss of human agency. Dystopian narratives in literature and visual arts can illuminate the darker aspects of AI technology with a sense of urgency, prompting audiences to consider the ramifications of unchecked AI development. Such representations can reveal the underlying biases in algorithmic design or the pernicious effects of automation on the workforce, highlighting the human cost of technological progress. By fostering critical discourse, art plays an instrumental role in navigating the ethical landscape of AI, urging society to confront and engage with the challenges that it presents. The intersection of art and AI can pave the way for innovative collaborations that redefine creative boundaries. As artists begin to incorporate AI technologies into their work, the possibilities for new aesthetic experiences open up. These collaborations can result in novel forms of expression that dynamically challenge the concept of authorship and creativity in an age increasingly defined by machine learning. Generative art created through AI algorithms invites viewers to contemplate the nature of creativity itself—who is the true author when a machine is involved in the creative process? This dialogue not only enriches the artistic landscape but also sparks broader discussions about the unique capabilities of humans versus machines. The partnership between art and AI prompts a reexamination of human identity in a tech-driven future, demonstrating that art is essential in understanding not just AI, but what it means to be human in an increasingly automated world.

XV. CASE STUDIES OF AI IMPLEMENTATION

In recent years, the integration of AI into healthcare systems has emerged as a significant case study for examining the impacts of AI implementation. Healthcare providers are increasingly utilizing AI algorithms for diagnostic purposes, enabling them to analyze vast amounts of medical data far more efficiently than human counterparts. AI systems like IBM's Watson have demonstrated remarkable accuracy in identifying diseases from patient records and imaging results. This technological advancement not only expedites the diagnostic process but also enhances the potential for personalized treatment plans, tailoring healthcare to individual patient needs. The reliance on AI in such a sensitive field prompts critical ethical considerations, particularly regarding data privacy and the potential biases inherent in algorithmic decision-making. As healthcare providers adopt these technologies, it is imperative to maintain transparency and accountability, ensuring that the benefits of AI do not eclipse the ethical responsibilities that the medical profession upholds. Another noteworthy example of AIs transformative power can be found in the financial sector, where machine learning algorithms are being employed to assess credit risk and automate trading. Financial institutions leverage sophisticated AI models to analyze consumer data, identifying patterns that can predict defaults on loans more accurately than traditional methods. This predictive capability improves the overall risk management strategies of these organizations, allowing for more informed lending practices and pricing strategies. Robo-advisors are reshaping investment portfolios by using AI to analyze market trends and provide personalized advice to investors, democratizing access to wealth management services. Nevertheless, the deployment of these technologies raises profound questions about the potential displacement of jobs and the necessity of regulatory frameworks to ensure fairness and equity. As we navigate the complexities of AI in finance, a balance must be struck between embracing innovation and safeguarding the human elements that underpin trust and integrity in financial dealings. The retail industry serves as yet another compelling case study that highlights the multifaceted applications of AI technology. Companies like Amazon have revolutionized the shopping experience by leveraging AI for inventory management, customer recommendations, and dynamic pricing strategies. Machine learning algorithms analyze shopping behaviors and preferences, offering personalized product suggestions that enhance customer engagement. AI-driven analytics improve supply chain efficiency, reducing waste and ensuring that products are stocked according to demand fluctuations. This rapid adoption of AI technologies also presents challenges, particularly concerning the ethical implications of consumer surveillance and data collection practices. As retailers collect and analyze vast troves of consumer data, the potential for misuse increases, necessitating robust privacy policies to protect consumers. Thus, while the implementation of AI in retail has streamlined operations and enhanced user experiences, it also raises essential questions about privacy rights, consumer autonomy, and the ethical boundaries of data utilization in the pursuit of profit.

Successful AI Projects in Various Industries

Innovative applications of AI are reshaping industries, demonstrating the transformative potential of this technology in practical settings. The healthcare sector stands out as a particularly salient example, where AI-driven algorithms are improving patient outcomes and operational efficiencies. Machine learning models analyze complex medical data to assist in diagnosing conditions ranging from cancer to rare diseases, often with greater precision than human practitioners. IBMs Watson Health utilizes vast databases of clinical information to provide oncologists with evidence-based treatment options tailored to individual patients. Such advancements not only enhance diagnostic accuracy but also liberate medical professionals from the burdens of administrative tasks, allowing them to focus on patient care. As hospitals adopt AI tools, they have reported improved patient satisfaction, reduced errors, and significant cost savings, compelling evidence of the potential benefits that can emerge when AI and healthcare intersect. Similarly, the financial industry has embraced AI to enhance decision-making and risk assessment, fundamentally altering how firms operate. Algorithms designed for predictive analytics enable institutions to detect fraudulent activities in real-time, mitigating potential losses and enhancing consumer trust. American Express employs machine learning algorithms to scrutinize transaction patterns and flag anomalies indicative of fraud, effectively pushing the boundaries of security in financial transactions. AI in investment banking allows for the analysis of market trends and consumer behavior at unprecedented speeds, leading to more informed trading strategies. This integration of AI fosters a proactive rather than reactive form of risk management, ensuring that firms are better equipped to navigate the volatility of markets. As these transformations unfold, financial institutions are not only achieving higher profit margins but also reshaping customer experiences— evidence that AIs impact extends far beyond mere efficiency. Manufacturing also stands at the forefront of AI implementation, with smart factories revolutionizing production processes. By incorporating AI technologies such as robotics, machine learning, and the Internet of Things (IoT), companies are achieving heightened levels of efficiency and productivity. Siemens has developed AI systems that monitor machinery performance through predictive maintenance, reducing downtime and operational costs. The ability to analyze real-time data enables manufacturers to anticipate equipment failures before they occur, fostering a more resilient production environment. AI-powered supply chain management tools optimize logistics by forecasting demand and adjusting inventory levels dynamically. This level of responsiveness not only minimizes waste but also aligns production capacities with market needs, creating a more sustainable industrial ecosystem. As manufacturers continue to explore and implement AI solutions, they cultivate a landscape of innovation that promises to redefine efficiency, competitiveness, and sustainability in the industrial sector.

Failures and Lessons Learned

Navigating the intricate realm of technological advancement, society has encountered a myriad of challenges that illustrate the fragility of human foresight. The rapid evolution of AI has presented unprecedented opportunities while simultaneously exposing significant vulnerabilities in collective understanding. Historical examples, such as the introduction of social media algorithms that inadvertently magnified misinformation, high-light the unintended consequences of deploying powerful tech-nologies without fully comprehending their societal impact. As AI continues to permeate various aspects of life, the lessons drawn from these failures underscore the necessity for rigorous ethical scrutiny and proactive governance. The intersection of innovation and responsibility becomes increasingly critical, as mishaps not only erode public trust but also pose existential risks to societal harmony and individual privacy. In the quest for progress, acknowledging failure serves as a cornerstone for sus-tainable growth. The integration of AI into industries like healthcare and transportation has often been met with skepti-cism due to early missteps, such as flawed predictive models or biased algorithms that disproportionately affect marginalized groups. These shortcomings have led to widespread calls for greater transparency, inclusivity, and rigorous testing in AI de-velopment. By confronting past failures head-on, developers and policymakers can cultivate an environment of continuous improvement and innovation that prioritizes ethical considera-tions. Recognizing and addressing failures can catalyze trans-formative change, fostering a symbiotic relationship between humanity and technology. This iterative process not only enhances technological efficacy but also ensures a more equitable approach to implementation, allowing society to learn from its mistakes and adapt to future challenges. The journey toward an AI-empowered future is fraught with complexities that demand an agile and informed response from all stakeholders. As societal reliance on technology deepens, the interplay of ethical frameworks, regulatory measures, and public sentiment will shape the landscape of AI development. The failure to integrate diverse perspectives and experiences into the technological narrative has often led to a narrow understanding of the potential ramifications of AI. By embracing inclusivity and interdisciplinary collaboration, a more robust foundation can be established, one that mitigates risks while maximizing benefits. As humanity stands on the precipice of transformative change, the importance of fostering resilience through learned experiences cannot be overstated. These lessons pave the way for a future where AI serves not only as a tool for advancement but also as an ally in the pursuit of a more just and equitable society.

Comparative Analysis of Global AI Strategies

In exploring the various global strategies for artificial intelligence, one cannot overlook the stark differences between nations regarding their regulatory frameworks and developmental priorities. The European Union advocates for a comprehensive regulatory approach, centering on ethical considerations and human rights. This regulatory framework aims to ensure that AI technologies align with societal values, focusing heavily on accountability and transparency. In contrast, the United States tends to promote a more laissez-faire approach, prioritizing innovation and market growth over stringent regulations. This divergence illustrates how differing national priorities influence AIs trajectory, affecting issues such as data privacy, algorithmic bias, and the displacement of labor. Countries like China, Pursue aggressive state-driven initiatives to dominate the global AI landscape, emphasizing technological supremacy and economic control. An examination of the financial investments allocated to AI reveals another crucial layer in understanding global strategies. In Silicon Valley, venture capital has been a crucial driver of AI startups, enabling rapid experimentation and scaling of cutting-edge technologies. The United States funding habits encourage a risk-taking culture that fosters innovation but often overlooks broader societal implications. In contrast, nations such as Japan take a more measured approach, prioritizing public investment in research and development. This government-led model encourages collaboration between academia and industry, allowing for a long-term vision that may mitigate the ethical concerns frequently sidelined by faster-paced capitalist models. Meanwhile, the European Union seeks to secure funding through collective initiatives, emphasizing policies aimed at enhancing collaboration among member states to achieve shared technological goals. This complex interplay of funding styles not only influences the nature of AI development but also raises questions about how each region addresses the ethical dilemmas posed by these advancements. The cultural underpinnings of each country's approach to AI also warrant consideration, as they directly impact the acceptance and integration of these technologies within society. In cultures that emphasize collectivism, such as those found in many Asian countries, AI solutions may be received as tools for societal good, aimed at enhancing overall welfare and efficiency. Conversely, individualistic societies, like those in the West, may raise more concerns regarding personal privacy and autonomy, reflecting deeper societal anxieties about control and surveillance. Public perception of AI can significantly affect policy decisions; in nations where the populace embraces technological advancement, governments may have the leeway to integrate AI more deeply into everyday life without facing substantial resistance. Where skepticism prevails, as seen in parts of Europe and North America, policymakers may tread cautiously, particularly in relation to surveillance technologies and data harvesting practices. Understanding these cultural narratives is essential for crafting policies that resonate with citizens while guiding the responsible deployment of AI.

XVI. THE ROLE OF EDUCATION IN AI LITERACY

In the contemporary landscape of technological innovation, the growing integration of AI into various sectors emphasizes the necessity for a populace equipped with robust AI literacy. Educational systems play a pivotal role in shaping this literacy by embedding AI concepts into curricula. Such initiatives not only demystify AIs functionalities but also provide students with the critical analytical skills required to assess its implications. Enhanced understanding fosters a proactive approach among learners, encouraging them to engage with AI technologies thoughtfully rather than passively consuming them. By incorporating subjects like data science, coding, and ethics related to AI into traditional education, institutions empower students to navigate an increasingly complex digital environment while cultivating a sense of responsibility towards their interactions with technology. The quest for widespread AI literacy necessitates ongoing education beyond formal schooling, particularly for adults who may feel the impacts of AI on their respective fields. Continuous professional development programs and workshops tailored to various industries can alleviate fears surrounding job displacement and empower employees with the skills needed to adapt to new AI-enhanced roles. By facilitating lifelong learning, these initiatives ensure that individuals remain competitive and capable in a rapidly evolving job market. Collaboration between educational institutions, corporations, and technology developers can create a comprehensive ecosystem that promotes knowledge sharing and innovation. This synergy not only enriches the learning experience but also paves the way for a future workforce that is not just consumers of AI technologies but also informed contributors to its ethical development. Fostering AI literacy is intrinsic to addressing the ethical dilemmas that arise alongside its deployment. An educated populace can critically engage with the social, cultural, and moral questions posed by AI systems, thereby encouraging the development of guidelines and policies that reflect diverse perspectives. Discussions about privacy, bias, and accountability become more nuanced when informed by a foundational understanding of AIs complexities. In this manner, education acts as a bulwark against the potential misuse of AI and promotes a culture where ethical considerations are paramount in the development and application of technology. Instilling a robust sense of AI literacy serves not merely as a mechanism for advancement but as a vital component of a conscientious society capable of harnessing the transformative power of AI for the collective good.

Curriculum Development for AI Understanding

As the rapid evolution of AI continues to redefine societal norms, a pressing need for comprehensive curricula centered around AI understanding emerges. Incorporating interdisciplinary methodologies into educational frameworks can enhance critical thinking and equip students with the skills necessary to navigate an increasingly automated world. Effective curriculum development should leverage insights from computer science, ethics, philosophy, and sociology to create a multifaceted approach. Students must not only grasp the technical aspects of AI but also engage with the ethical implications and societal impacts of these technologies. By integrating these diverse fields, curricula can prepare students to participate in meaningful discussions surrounding AIs role in society while fostering an understanding of underlying algorithms and data structures that govern machine learning processes. In aligning educational goals with the demands of a technologically advanced society, it becomes essential to focus on experiential learning. Project-based assignments, internships, and collaborative efforts with tech industries can provide invaluable hands-on experiences that bridge theoretical knowledge with real-world application. These immersive activities cultivate an environment where students can critically analyze AI technologies while understanding their practical implications. Simulating AI-driven projects allows learners to confront complex challenges related to bias in algorithms or data privacy concerns firsthand. Such experiences not only deepen their understanding but also encourage innovative problem-solving skills essential for future leaders in the AI field. Consequently, when curriculum development prioritizes experiential learning, it empowers students to become proactive contributors to AI discourse, capable of navigating both its promises and pitfalls. A pivotal aspect of curriculum development lies in fostering an inclusive learning environment that embraces diverse perspectives. Incorporating voices from various cultural, economic, and gender backgrounds can enrich discussions surrounding AI and ensure a more equitable understanding of its ramifications. When students engage with a wide range of viewpoints, they become better equipped to address the complex ethical dilemmas posed by AI technologies, such as surveillance and privacy concerns. Promoting diversity in AI education enables the challenge of existing biases, often reflective of narrow perspectives prevalent in technology development. By prioritizing inclusivity and critical dialogue in educational settings, curricula not only illuminate the multifaceted nature of AI but also cultivate responsible citizens adept at shaping a future where technology enhances human potential rather than undermining it.

Promoting STEM Education

In an age dominated by rapid technological advancement, the emphasis on STEM (science, technology, engineering, and mathematics) education cannot be overstated. As the landscape of work continuously evolves due to AI and automation, a solid foundation in STEM equips students with critical skills essential for navigating this shifting terrain. Educational institutions play a pivotal role in fostering interest in these fields from an early age, ensuring that students not only understand theoretical concepts but also possess practical skills applicable in real-world situations. Initiatives that promote hands-on learning, such as coding camps and robotics competitions, can ignite curiosity and inspire the next generation of innovators. By embracing an interdisciplinary approach that connects STEM subjects to everyday life, educators can cultivate a mindset that values inquiry, creativity, and problem-solving—key components for thriving in an AI-driven economy. The importance of diversity within STEM fields also merits discussion, as a broad array of perspectives can lead to groundbreaking innovations. Unfortunately, women and minorities remain underrepresented in many STEM-related occupations, suggesting systemic barriers need addressing. Active participation in promoting STEM education must prioritize inclusivity and equitable access for all students. Mentorship programs, scholarships, and community outreach initiatives specifically targeting underrepresented groups can help dismantle these barriers and foster a more diverse talent pool. Such endeavors are not only morally imperative but strategically beneficial; diverse teams drive innovation by offering varied viewpoints that lead to unique solutions to complex problems. As the world increasingly relies on technology and data-driven decision-making, it is crucial to empower a wide spectrum of voices that can contribute to the development of ethical and effective AI systems. Preparation for the future goes beyond simply enhancing technical skills; it encompasses nurturing critical thinking, adaptability, and ethical considerations in human interactions with technology. As AI continues to shape an interconnected global society, it is imperative that students learn to critically evaluate the implications of their work. Educational curricula must integrate discussions around the ethical use of technology, emphasizing the responsibility that comes with innovation. By encouraging students to engage with pressing societal issues—such as privacy, bias in algorithms, and the environmental impact of technological advancement—they can better understand the broader implications of their contributions. This holistic approach prepares them not only to excel in their future careers but also to become conscientious citizens who can thoughtfully navigate the complexities of an increasingly tech-driven world. In promoting STEM education, a focus on ethics and critical engagement ensures that technological advancements align with the fundamental values of humanity.

Lifelong Learning in the Age of AI

In the dynamic landscape shaped by artificial intelligence, the concept of lifelong learning has become not just beneficial, but essential for individuals seeking to thrive. As AI technologies advance and redefine job roles across numerous industries, the need for continuous education ensures adaptability in an ever-evolving job market. Traditional educational paradigms are rapidly being upended, as the skills demanded today may become obsolete tomorrow. Jobs that rely heavily on repetitive tasks can be automated, benefitting those who have invested in acquiring critical thinking and problem-solving skills instead. Consequently, individuals must cultivate a mindset geared towards ongoing education, embracing platforms that foster skill enhancement outside conventional classrooms. Empowered by online resources and more accessible tools, learners can curate personalized learning experiences that reflect both current trends and individual aspirations, positioning themselves competitively amidst technological shifts. The integration of AI into various sectors opens avenues for innovative learning methods that weren't possible before. Adaptive learning technologies, which tailor educational content to the needs and learning pace of individual students, illustrate how AI can enhance educational experiences. With data-driven insights, AI can identify gaps in understanding, prompting targeted interventions that can vastly improve the retention and application of knowledge. This personalization fosters a deeper engagement with learning, as students are not just passive recipients of information but active participants in their educational journeys. Professionals can utilize AI-powered platforms to access just-in-time learning, acquiring relevant skills that align with immediate job requirements or future career goals. In this way, lifelong learning fortified by AI empowers individuals not only to respond to the demands of their current roles, but also to anticipate future industry transformations. The role of lifelong learning in an AI-augmented world underscores a broader societal shift towards ongoing personal and professional development. As learning becomes a continuous, lifetime endeavor, emphasis on collaboration and knowledge sharing emerges as integral components of this journey. Communities and workplaces are increasingly fostering environments that encourage collective learning, promoting mentorship and peer-to-peer education. This collaborative ethos benefits individuals by providing social support and enhancing motivation, while also cultivating diverse skills that can lead to innovation and growth across sectors. As AI systems become more intertwined with human capabilities, ethical considerations around the future of work and knowledge dissemination will necessitate ongoing dialogue and critical thinking. Thus, embracing lifelong learning not only prepares individuals to navigate the complexities of AI integration but also counters the potential risks of technological displacement and inequality, fostering a more informed and resilient society.

XVII. AI AND THE FUTURE OF CREATIVITY

The integration of AI into the creative process prompts a profound examination of originality and authorship. As algorithms become adept at generating art, music, and literature, questions arise about the essence of creativity itself. Traditionally viewed as an inherently human trait, creativity involves not merely the act of creating but also the nuanced interplay of emotion, experience, and intent. With AI systems capable of producing works that mimic human styles and emotions, the boundaries of what constitutes true creativity are increasingly blurred. This technological evolution challenges the notion that creativity is strictly a byproduct of human consciousness, prompting a reevaluation of the roles both AI and human artists play in the cultural landscape. This intersection raises the possibility of redefining artistic value in a world where machines can contribute their own interpretations alongside human input. The collaboration between AI and human creatives can yield innovative outcomes that neither could achieve in isolation. By leveraging AI's ability to analyze vast datasets and identify patterns, artists and writers are discovering new avenues of inspiration and expression. Musicians are utilizing AI to compose complex symphonies that blend multiple genres, while visual artists are creating immersive installations that incorporate real-time data analytics. Such collaborations empower creatives to transcend traditional boundaries, fostering an environment ripe for experimentation. This co-creative relationship, Necessitates an ongoing dialogue about the ethical implications of using AI-generated content. Who holds the copyright when a piece is produced collaboratively? How are the sociocultural impacts addressed when AI systems learn from biased datasets? These questions serve as critical touchpoints for the discourse surrounding AI's role in creative industries. While the potential benefits of AI in fostering creativity are groundbreaking, apprehension about its implications cannot be overlooked. There exists a palpable fear that reliance on AI could lead to a homogenization of creative expression, undermining the unique perspectives that human creators bring to their work. The risk of commodification looms large; if AI-generated art floods the market, it may diminish the value assigned to human-made masterpieces. As AI continues to evolve, the possibility arises that society may prioritize algorithmically produced content over genuine human experiences, leading to a disconnect between art and its viewers. To navigate this complex terrain, it is essential for stakeholders in the creative industries to engage proactively with the technology, establishing frameworks that honor human creativity while embracing the potential of AI. By doing so, they can ensure that the future of creativity remains a rich tapestry woven from both human and artificial threads.

AI in Artistic Expression

The emergence of AI as a collaborator in the realm of artistic expression marks a significant paradigm shift. Historically, artists have relied on their subjective experiences and emotions to create works that resonate with audiences on a deeply personal level. The integration of AI tools enables the exploration of new dimensions in this creative process. Algorithms can analyze vast amounts of data, recognizing patterns and trends that might elude human perception. Such capabilities not only augment the creative toolkit available to artists but also challenge traditional notions of authorship. When algorithms generate innovative visual art or compose music, questions arise about the nature of creativity itself. Can an AI truly create, or is it merely processing inputs from the vast human cultural tapestry? This convergence prompts a reevaluation of what it means to be an artist in an increasingly digital landscape, pushing the boundaries of human creativity into uncharted territory. The collaboration between humans and AI in artistic endeavors raises multifaceted ethical dilemmas that necessitate careful consideration. As artists harness AI technologies, the potential for misuse or the commodification of art comes into sharper focus. The rapid proliferation of AI-generated imagery or music might dilute the perceived value of traditional art forms, as consumers may gravitate toward the novelty and efficiency offered by machines. These shifts could lead to a homogenization of creative outputs, as algorithms tend to draw from existing data and trends, thereby risking the loss of unique, individualized expression. The issue of intellectual property becomes increasingly complex as shared ownership between human creators and artificial entities blurs the lines of originality and authorship. As we embrace AIs role in art, society must engage in dialogues that navigate these intricacies, ensuring that technology enhances rather than diminishes the human experience of creativity. Looking ahead, the interplay of AI and artistic expression invites a reimagining of cultural landscapes and fosters potential pathways for innovative collaboration. Rather than viewing AI as a replacement for human artistry, many creatives are beginning to see it as a partner that can inspire and push boundaries. Interactive installations and immersive experiences powered by AI challenge audiences to engage with art in new and dynamic ways. As artists experiment with AI-generated content alongside their own, they may uncover unique synergies that lead to entirely new genres or artistic movements. The infusion of AI into the arts not only enhances the creative palette available to artists but also provokes profound questions about the future of culture in an age of technological advancement. By embracing a symbiotic relationship between human creativity and artificial intelligence, society can foster a richer, more diverse artistic expression that reflects the complexities of the human experience within an increasingly automated world.

The Role of AI in Music and Film

Technological innovation has fundamentally altered the landscape of artistic creation, particularly in music and film. By harnessing the capabilities of artificial intelligence, creators are now able to explore uncharted territory, producing works that challenge traditional understandings of artistry and authorship. AIs role extends beyond mere production, as tools such as generative algorithms and machine learning enable artists to analyze vast datasets of existing works. This capacity allows for the exploration of patterns and styles that may remain inaccessible through human intuition alone. The result is a melding of human creativity and machine efficiency, culminating in projects that can be at once familiar and groundbreaking. As AI expands the boundaries of what's possible, it also raises the question of what it means to be an artist in an age where machines can replicate and innovate upon concepts that were once exclusively human. The integration of AI into music and film has sparked considerable debate regarding ownership, creativity, and the future of collaboration. In film, AI can assist in various aspects, from scriptwriting to casting predictions, ultimately streamlining the filmmaking process. This not only reduces time and costs but can also result in craftsman-like precision in editing and visual effects. Such advancements often lead to concerns about the dilution of human creativity. Critics argue that reliance on AI may reduce the authenticity of artistic expression, as films produced through algorithmic processes might cater excessively to market trends, compromising the individuality of the creator. Similarly, in music, AI-generated compositions can mimic the styles of legendary artists, posing challenges to the traditional conception of originality and copyright. This blend of innovation and imitation creates a provocative dialogue about the essence of creativity and the evolving role of human artists in a digital milieu. The proliferation of AI in the creative industries prompts profound ethical considerations, particularly regarding the impact on employment and cultural production. As AI continues to streamline various creative processes, skilled professionals in music and film may face significant challenges in job security and industry relevance. While AI can augment creativity and efficiency, it also calls into question the lived experiences and perspectives that human artists bring to their work. The concern grows that algorithm-driven content could lead to homogenized outputs, effectively reducing diversity in artistic expression and cultural representation. Such a trend could diminish the richness of cultural narratives and erode the distinctiveness of human-made art forms. As society grapples with these implications, the discourse surrounding AI in music and film must extend beyond mere excitement and technological advancement, focusing instead on the ethical frameworks that must accompany such innovation to safeguard the essence of human creativity in an increasingly automated world.

Collaboration Between Artists and AI

The intersection of creativity and technology is being redefined by the collaboration between artists and artificial intelligence. This partnership presents an innovative amalgamation of human intuition and machine learning, fostering a landscape where traditional artistic boundaries are continually expanded. Generative art, created through algorithms, exemplifies how AI can imitate or even enhance human creativity. With the ability to analyze extensive databases of visual aesthetics and techniques, AI can propose novel artistic designs that might not emerge from a human mind alone. This collaboration empowers artists to push their creative limits and explore new dimensions of expression that blend human emotion and algorithmic precision, ultimately leading to unprecedented artistic movements. Despite the benefits of artistic collaboration with AI, significant concerns arise regarding authorship, originality, and the essence of creativity itself. The conversation surrounding intellectual property becomes complex when art is generated or significantly influenced by algorithms. Artists risk losing their unique voices as AI systems potentially eclipse human contributions. The dialogue around what constitutes artistic merit takes on new dimensions, with critics questioning whether art produced by AI can genuinely possess the intrinsic emotions and experiences characteristic of human creativity. This philosophical dilemma challenges artists to reflect on their roles and responsibilities in an age where technology plays an increasingly prominent role in shaping their work, inviting new discussions about the meaning of agency in the artistic process. Looking toward the future, the collaboration between human artists and AI holds transformative potential but also prompts essential ethical inquiries. As machines become more sophisticated, the risk of devaluation of human artistic expression increases. Yet, there are opportunities for technology to democratize art-making, allowing a wider array of voices to be heard and appreciated. Initiatives that involve community-based projects and AI can encourage participation from individuals who may not have had access to traditional artistic avenues. As artists continue to explore the capacities and limitations of AI, a critical dialogue must ensue surrounding the preservation of authenticity and the cultivation of creative communities in a technological landscape. Embracing the synergies between human ingenuity and AI could ultimately enrich our understanding of art's cultural significance while ensuring that humanity remains central to the creative narrative.

XVIII. THE IMPACT OF AI ON MENTAL HEALTH

The proliferation of AI within therapeutic contexts has led to significant changes in how individuals manage their mental health. AI-driven applications now provide users with 24/7 access to mental health resources, including chatbots and virtual therapists capable of assessing symptoms and delivering tailored interventions. These tools often utilize natural language processing to understand user sentiments and provide relevant support, making mental health care more accessible, especially for those who might face barriers in traditional settings. While such advancements democratize access, they also raise questions about the effectiveness and reliability of automated solutions. The absence of human empathy and nuanced understanding in AI interactions could lead to oversimplification of complex emotional issues, thus hampering the depth of care that individuals receive. A reliance on technology for mental health support may inadvertently foster a sense of isolation or disconnection, as users may treat AI systems as substitutes for authentic human engagement. The presence of AI in our daily lives shapes societal perceptions of mental health and well-being. The normalization of AI companions, often marketed as tools for alleviating loneliness, can inadvertently diminish human-to-human relationships, complicating social dynamics. As people increasingly interact with intelligent systems, there is a danger of becoming desensitized to genuine emotional experiences, leading to a potential decline in empathetic capacities. This shift could paradoxically exacerbate mental health issues, as individuals feel less inclined to seek real human connections, relying instead on the superficial engagement provided by AI. The pervasive integration of AI into social media algorithms and content dissemination can contribute to distorted self-perceptions and unrealistic comparisons with curated online personas. Consequently, individuals may grapple with heightened anxiety, depression, or other mental health concerns, influenced by the very tools designed to support them. Nevertheless, the evolving landscape of AI offers the potential for enhanced mental health interventions when harnessed responsibly. Future developments in AI could focus on personalized medicine, where algorithms analyze vast datasets to identify the most effective treatment modalities for individuals based on their unique psychological profiles. Incorporating ethical considerations into AI design can emphasize compassion and understanding, allowing these technologies to serve as complementary rather than replacement options in mental healthcare. By fostering collaboration between human practitioners and AI systems, the therapeutic process could benefit from the efficiency and accessibility provided by technology while maintaining the critical, empathetic core of human interaction. A deliberate approach to integrating AI into mental health care can lead to a future where individuals receive holistic support that honors both technological advancements and the deeply rooted need for human connection.

AI in Psychological Support and Therapy

Emerging technologies increasingly navigate complex emotional landscapes, enhancing psychological support mechanisms through AI (AI). The implementation of AI in therapeutic contexts enables a level of accessibility that traditional methods often struggle to achieve. AI-driven chatbots and mental health apps provide immediate support to individuals in distress, transcending geographical and socioeconomic barriers. Such interventions can serve as first points of contact, effectively triaging mental health needs and directing users to appropriate resources. The ability to offer assistance round the clock aligns with the fast-paced lives of many individuals today, who may be unable to seek help during conventional office hours. Consequently, AI has the potential to democratize mental health care, ensuring that support is not a privilege reserved for those who can afford it but a universal right accessible to all. The integration of AI into psychological support systems raises several critical considerations regarding the nature of therapy itself. One of the major benefits of AI platforms is their data-driven approach, which allows for the personalization of treatment plans that adapt based on user interactions and feedback. This adaptive capability presents an intriguing shift from traditional, one-size-fits-all therapeutic models toward more tailored solutions that consider individual experiences and preferences. While the data analytics employed can enhance efficacy, it simultaneously invites scrutiny over privacy and ethical concerns, as sensitive information is collected and analyzed. Therapists must remain vigilant in balancing technology's benefits against the risks of dehumanization and data exploitation. Understanding these dynamics will be crucial in navigating the evolving landscape of mental health support. Equally important is the acknowledgment of AIs limitations in the realm of human emotions and subjective experiences. Although AI can simulate empathetic responses and provide structured support, the absence of genuine human connection remains a significant gap in the therapeutic process. Therapy is not merely about the content relayed but is deeply rooted in the relational bonds between therapist and client. The nuanced understanding that comes from shared human experiences and emotions is challenging for AI to replicate, potentially leading to superficial interactions. Thus, while AI has made remarkable strides in supporting mental health initiatives, it should not be seen as a replacement for traditional therapy. A blended approach, combining AIs accessibility with human therapists insights, may provide the most effective solution to this rapidly evolving challenge in psychological care.

The Effects of AI on Human Relationships

As the integration of AI into daily life continues to accelerate, some researchers caution that it may sow discord in human relationships. While initial interactions with AI can be engaging, fostering a sense of companionship and support, there is a risk that reliance on these technologies may erode human connections. For many, AI-driven platforms offer convenience and efficiency, facilitating communication and task management. This convenience can lead to decreased face-to-face interactions, potentially weakening the fabric of social bonds. By prioritizing conversations with machines over those with people, individuals may inadvertently neglect the emotional nuances and shared experiences that underpin meaningful relationships. Thus, while AI may serve as a useful tool, it is imperative to recognize its potential to supplant rather than enhance interpersonal connections. The shift toward AI-mediated interactions raises concerns about authenticity and emotional intelligence in relationships. When individuals engage with AI systems that mimic sentiment and understanding, they may find themselves in a paradoxical situation where emotional depth is manufactured rather than organically fostered. This can create an illusion of connection, leaving individuals craving the genuine empathy and human understanding that technology struggles to replicate. Younger generations, who are increasingly accustomed to digital communication, might experience a skewed perception of relationships, valuing efficiency over emotional resonance. In light of this transformation, traditional forms of communication and conflict resolution may suffer, leading to superficial relationships devoid of the richness that characterizes human interactions. As individuals become more comfortable with artificial companionship, the essential skills necessary for nurturing authentic relationships could become endangered. The influence of AI on human relationships is multifaceted, requiring critical reflection on how these technologies shape social interactions. While AI offers unprecedented opportunities for connection and convenience, it simultaneously poses a threat to the depth and quality of human relationships. Encouraging a balanced approach that integrates AI without overshadowing the human elements of empathy and emotional engagement is paramount. By fostering awareness of the potential pitfalls associated with excessive reliance on technology, society can strive to create environments where human relationships remain a priority. Rather than viewing AI solely as a tool that facilitates communication, it is essential to approach its integration thoughtfully, ensuring that the values inherent in human connections continue to thrive in an increasingly digitized world.

Addressing Mental Health Challenges in an AI World

Technological advancements, particularly in artificial intelligence, are fundamentally reshaping our daily lives and interactions, and this transformation extends deeply into the realm of mental health. With the proliferation of digital solutions, individuals now have unprecedented access to resources designed to aid mental well-being. AI-driven applications can provide cognitive behavioral therapy, mood tracking, and even instant access to support networks. These innovations are especially crucial in environments where traditional clinical resources are limited, thereby democratizing mental health support. The technology's efficacy hinges not only on its accessibility but also on the implementation strategies adopted by developers and health professionals. The challenge lies in ensuring that these tools are scientifically validated and empathetic, fostering a connection that reinforces users mental health rather than relegating them to mechanistic interactions devoid of human warmth. The emergence of AI in mental health also amplifies existing ethical concerns surrounding privacy and data security. As users engage with AI frameworks, they invariably disclose sensitive personal information that, if not handled with care, can lead to significant consequences. This presents a dual challenge: on one hand, the integration of advanced algorithms could lead to tailored therapeutic interventions that are highly effective, yet on the other, this requires safeguarding against breaches that could exploit individuals' vulnerabilities. The establishment of robust ethical guidelines and standards is essential to protect users while enhancing the benefits of AI in mental health care. Clear communication about the limitations of such technologies is necessary to manage expectations and ensure users retain a sense of agency, thereby preventing dependence on automated systems that might inadvertently undermine the human element essential to therapeutic success. As society continues to integrate AI into mental health treatment, fostering an inclusive framework is essential for addressing the diverse challenges faced by various populations. Marginalized communities, in particular, often encounter heightened barriers to accessing mental health resources. Through the strategic application of AI, solutions could be devised that specifically cater to these demographics, ensuring that language, cultural context, and unique experiences are considered in treatment options. This ambition necessitates collaboration among technologists, mental health professionals, and community leaders to design platforms that resonate with users lived experiences. Thus, the goal should not merely center on technological innovation but rather on cultivating a holistic network that prioritizes human dignity and connection. Embracing this ethos could lead to a future where AI not only serves as a tool for assistance but also as a catalyst for social change in mental health advocacy and accessibility.

XIX. THE GLOBAL AI RACE

Amidst escalating technological advancements, nations around the world are jostling for supremacy in the realm of artificial intelligence. This pursuit reflects not only a quest for economic dominance but also a strategic drive to bolster national security. Countries like the United States and China are heavily investing in AI research and infrastructure, recognizing that the nation that attains superiority in AI capabilities could potentially dictate global standards and frameworks. The competitive landscape is characterized by a sense of urgency, as governments race to harness AIs transformative potential, viewing it as a means to foster innovation, improve efficiencies, and gain geopolitical leverage. This pursuit, Is not merely a matter of technological advancement; it highlights a deeper ideological battle over governance, ethics, and human rights, raising fundamental questions about how AI will shape societal values and political structures. At the core of this race lies a complex interplay of investment in research, talent acquisition, and international collaboration. Many countries are developing strategic plans to nurture homegrown talent while also striving to attract leading AI experts from around the globe. The establishment of research labs, AI incubators, and academic partnerships reflects a recognition that collaboration could yield accelerated progress in AI development. Nations are increasingly aware that fostering public-private partnerships can amplify the impact of investments in the sector. The implications of these initiatives extend beyond national borders, considering how advancements in AI might ultimately be utilized for global challenges, such as climate change and public health crises. Nevertheless, these co-operative efforts are often complicated by protective policies and competitive inclinations, underscoring a paradox where collaboration could also lead to tensions over intellectual property and technological espionage. The consequences of the global AI race will reverberate through multiple dimensions of human life, both positively and negatively. On one hand, the quest for advanced AI could drive unprecedented innovations, potentially addressing some of the world's most pressing issues, such as efficient resource distribution and enhanced healthcare systems. The heightened competition may exacerbate existing inequalities, particularly if access to AI technologies becomes a privilege of the elite or the economically powerful. As nations prioritize AI development, ethical considerations regarding surveillance, algorithmic bias, and autonomous weaponry may take a backseat to the race itself, escalating existential risks. As we move deeper into this era marked by rapid AI evolution, it is critical to cultivate a balanced approach that mitigates risks while ensuring that the benefits of AI advancements are equitably distributed across society. Consequently, the success of AI will not merely hinge on technological breakthroughs but on the frameworks established to govern their use effectively.

Competition Among Nations for AI Dominance

In the contemporary landscape, the race for supremacy in AI has intertwined technological advancement with national power dynamics. Nations are increasingly recognizing that AI capabilities directly influence economic competitiveness and military strength. In this context, countries like the United States, China, and members of the European Union are pouring resources into AI research and talent cultivation. This competition manifests itself not only in the domains of technological innovation but also in strategic partnerships and international collaborations. Control over AI technologies fosters broader geopolitical leverage, underscoring the urgency of attaining breakthroughs in machine learning, neural networks, and autonomous systems. As countries jockey for position, the implications extend far beyond mere economic gain, framing AI as a critical element of national security and global influence. Strategic investments in AI research are similarly reshaping the global workforce landscape. Nations are not only focusing on technological advancements but also prioritizing education systems that prepare future generations for an AI-driven world. In the United States, Educational reforms aim to cultivate skills directly applicable to AI and related fields. Conversely, countries like China are fostering an aggressive push to integrate AI in various sectors, from manufacturing to healthcare, aiming to gain a competitive edge. The pursuit of AI dominance creates a ripple effect in labor markets, necessitating a re-evaluation of job sectors that could be disrupted by automation. The potential for job displacement fuels a broader discourse on ethical considerations surrounding AI development, compelling policymakers to create frameworks that address both economic and social repercussions. As nations strive for AI leadership, ethical considerations and global collaboration increasingly take center stage. The overwhelming pace of AI advancements raises concerns about misuse, privacy infringement, and potential military applications, which could catalyze unforeseen crises. Consequently, nations must prioritize not only competitive positioning but also cooperative frameworks and ethical standards to mitigate risks associated with AI technologies. This includes international dialogues and agreements aimed at regulating AI's development and deployment. It calls for inclusivity in AI governance that accounts for diverse perspectives, ensuring a balance between innovation and human rights. As nations continue their pursuit of AI advantages, the intersections of competition, ethics, and cooperation will define the trajectory of technological progress and its impact on society as a whole.

The Role of International Collaboration

In an era defined by rapid technological advancement, the necessity of international collaboration emerges as a critical theme in navigating the complexities introduced by AI (AI). Various nations possess unique strengths and resources, making the synergy of diverse contributions essential for tackling the multifaceted challenges that AI presents. The advancement of AI technologies often necessitates shared research capabilities, data pooling, and ethical frameworks that transcend national boundaries. When countries collaborate, they foster environments that not only accelerate innovation but also ensure that diverse perspectives are considered. This inclusion can help mitigate biases inherent in AI systems, ultimately leading to technology that serves a broader spectrum of humanity. Hence, the cooperation between nations becomes imperative, not only for enhancing technological capabilities but also for reinforcing equitable and just outcomes in AI applications. Establishing international standards and guidelines plays a pivotal role in the governance of AI technologies. Without a cooperative framework, the risk of a fragmented global landscape arises, characterized by uneven regulations and differing ethical standards. Such fragmentation can lead to scenarios where AIs benefits are disproportionately distributed, exacerbating global inequalities. Organizations like the United Nations and various global coalitions are actively engaged in discussions to formulate universally acceptable norms regarding AI usage. These efforts illustrate how collective policymaking can pave the way for sustainable and responsible AI development. When countries engage collaboratively, they can harmonize their regulations, share best practices, and create streamlined processes that ensure technological advancements contribute positively to global welfare. The establishment of international standards acts as a safeguard against potential abuses of AI technologies while promoting a unified approach toward beneficial outcomes. The educational and cultural exchanges facilitated by international collaboration also play a significant role in shaping a future where AI is used ethically and effectively. By pooling knowledge and experience across nations, stakeholders can foster a more nuanced understanding of the societal implications of AI. Collaborative initiatives encourage diverse voices, representing varied cultural contexts and ethical perspectives, to contribute to discussions about the role of technology in society. The integration of these diverse viewpoints can lead to a richer, more comprehensive dialogue about AIs potential impacts and the ethical dilemmas it may pose. International partnerships in education can help cultivate a global workforce equipped to address the challenges of rapidly evolving technologies. As a result, nurturing an internationally-minded generation of innovators and leaders can drive the responsible integration of AI into society, ultimately steering humanity toward a future marked by collective consideration and collaborative progress.

Ethical Standards in Global AI Development

As AI continues to advance at an unprecedented pace, ethical standards in its development are becoming increasingly vital. The implications of AI technology are vast, influencing sectors from healthcare to finance and impacting everyday interactions. Without a robust ethical framework, there is a risk of perpetuating biases, violating privacy, and inadvertently misusing AI capabilities. Consequently, it is imperative for international stakeholders—including governments, corporations, and independent organizations—to collaboratively establish guidelines that prioritize fairness, accountability, and transparency. An ethical approach to AI must consider not only potential benefits but also the societal consequences of AI deployment, ensuring that innovation is balanced with safeguarding human rights. The global nature of AI development complicates the establishment of ethical norms. Individual countries may possess disparate regulatory frameworks reflecting their cultural values, economic conditions, and political environments. This divergence can lead to significant ethical dilemmas, particularly when AI technologies cross borders, creating scenarios in which one nation's standards clash with another's. The use of surveillance AI may be viewed as an enhancement of security in one country, while in another, it could be regarded as an infringement on personal freedoms. International cooperation is crucial in cultivating a shared understanding of ethical guidelines that can foster innovation while simultaneously protecting individual rights. Ongoing dialogues among nations are essential to harmonizing these standards to facilitate responsible AI development. The challenge of enacting ethical standards in AI development is exacerbated by the rapid pace of technological advancements and the lack of comprehensive understanding among stakeholders. Many of the developers and corporations creating these technologies prioritize economic gains over ethical considerations, potentially leading to dilemmas that are addressed only after negative consequences arise. Proactive engagement—through interdisciplinary collaboration involving ethicists, technologists, lawmakers, and the public—can yield better solutions that integrate ethical considerations at the design stage of AI systems. Such an approach encourages the anticipation of ethical implications and the creation of adaptive frameworks capable of evolving alongside technological advancements. The integration of ethical standards in global AI development represents a critical step in ensuring that the transformative potential of technology serves humanity responsibly and equitably.

XX. AI AND THE ENVIRONMENT

As AI continues to advance at an unprecedented pace, its implications for environmental management are becoming increasingly evident. These technologies are redefining how we monitor, model, and mitigate the impacts of climate change. By leveraging machine learning algorithms, researchers can analyze vast datasets related to weather patterns, pollution levels, and biodiversity, resulting in improved forecasting and enhanced decision-making capabilities. AI is being employed to optimize energy consumption in smart grids, reducing greenhouse gas emissions while maintaining reliable power supplies. Autonomous drones are utilized for reforestation projects, enabling faster and more efficient planting of trees in areas affected by deforestation. These initiatives exemplify how AI can serve as a pivotal tool in combating environmental degradation, providing solutions that are not only innovative but also scalable across diverse ecosystems. Despite its potential benefits, the ecological footprint of AI technologies warrants critical examination. The energy demands associated with training large-scale AI models can be substantial, leading to considerable carbon emissions if not managed appropriately. The infrastructure required for data centers, particularly those powered by non-renewable energy sources, poses a significant challenge for sustainable development. The mining of raw materials for essential components in AI systems—such as semiconductors and batteries—can contribute to habitat destruction and resource depletion. Acknowledging these detrimental effects is crucial for developing more sustainable AI practices that prioritize environmental health. Researchers and policymakers must collaborate to establish guidelines that ensure responsible AI deployment, aiming to strike a balance between technological innovation and ecological stewardship. To pave the way for a harmonious relationship between AI and the environment, a multi-faceted approach is necessary, emphasizing education, policy reform, and community engagement. Instilling an awareness of environmental implications in AI curricula will equip future technologists with the ethical frameworks needed to prioritize sustainability in their projects. Policymakers should implement regulations promoting the use of renewable energy in data centers and incentivize industries to adopt greener AI solutions. Fostering community-driven initiatives that utilize AI for local environmental challenges can demonstrate the capacity of technology to enhance grassroots conservation efforts. By embracing an integrated strategy that champions sustainability alongside technological advancement, society can harness the transformative power of AI while safeguarding our planet for generations to come. This balance will determine whether AI becomes a catalyst for positive environmental change or a contributor to the ongoing ecological crisis.

Sustainable AI Practices

In the contemporary landscape of technological innovation, the rapid advancement of AI mandates a conscientious approach to its development and implementation. As organizations leverage AI to enhance productivity and drive competitiveness, attention must also focus on minimizing its ecological footprint. Sustainable AI practices aim to balance efficiency with environmental responsibility by optimizing the training and operation of AI systems. Strategies such as utilizing energy-efficient hardware, implementing improved algorithms that reduce computational demands, and exploring renewable energy sources are instrumental in lessening the environmental impact of AI technologies. When adopted widely, these approaches can not only mitigate carbon emissions associated with AI but also cultivate a broader climate-conscious culture within the tech sector. The journey towards sustainable AI transcends mere energy efficiency; it also encompasses socially responsible development practices. This means integrating ethical considerations throughout the lifecycle of AI applications, from inception to deployment and beyond. Organizations are now recognizing that sustainability must include not only environmental factors but also social equity and ethical governance. By prioritizing diverse and inclusive datasets, companies can avoid perpetuating biases in AI algorithms, thus ensuring that these systems serve humanity holistically. Engaging diverse stakeholders in the decision-making process is vital to the equitable deployment of AI technologies, enabling a more balanced approach that reflects the varied interests of society while addressing pressing ethical dilemmas. As the conversation around sustainable AI practices evolves, it is crucial to consider their implications on future innovations and society at large. The potential for AI to create value while also posing existential risks necessitates a proactive stance on regulation and oversight. Policymakers must collaborate with technologists and ethicists to establish frameworks that foster responsible AI development without stifling innovation. By crafting policies that encourage transparency and accountability, society can better govern the use of AI technologies and harness their power for the collective good. The pursuit of sustainable AI practices serves not only to alleviate environmental concerns but also to bolster ethical standards, guiding the trajectory of AI toward benefiting humanity as a whole, rather than a select few.

AI in Environmental Monitoring

The integration of AI into environmental monitoring represents a turning point in our ability to understand and respond to ecological challenges. Traditional methods of environmental assessment often rely on manual data collection, which can be both time-consuming and prone to human error. In contrast, AI technologies facilitate real-time data collection and analysis, enabling researchers to monitor environmental parameters more efficiently than ever before. Techniques such as remote sensing, powered by AI algorithms, allow for continuous observation of deforestation, urban sprawl, and natural disasters. By processing vast amounts of satellite imagery and sensor data, AI can identify patterns and anomalies that may go unnoticed through conventional monitoring methods, thereby amplifying our capacity to manage and protect ecosystems. This technological advancement not only enhances our understanding of environmental changes but also supports timely intervention strategies that could mitigate potential hazards. AIs predictive capabilities offer a proactive approach to environmental management. Machine learning models can analyze historical and real-time data to forecast ecological trends, such as climate fluctuations and species population dynamics. AI can predict the likelihood of invasive species spreading into new territories, enabling policymakers to take preventive measures. This anticipatory aspect enhances the resilience of ecosystems by facilitating informed decision-making and strategic resource allocation. By leveraging AI, environmental organizations can prioritize conservation efforts based on the likelihood of success and urgency, ensuring that limited resources are allocated where they will be most effective. The provision of actionable insights through AI not only improves environmental stewardship but also encourages collaboration across disciplines—uniting scientists, policymakers, and communities in a shared mission to tackle pressing environmental issues. Nevertheless, the reliance on AI in environmental monitoring raises significant ethical questions that demand careful consideration. As these intelligent systems become more embedded in ecological governance, concerns about data privacy, bias, and the dehumanization of decision-making processes emerge. The potential for algorithms to reinforce existing inequalities or misinterpret ecological data calls for a critical examination of the criteria and datasets used to train AI models. Ensuring transparency and accountability in how AI systems are developed and implemented is crucial for maintaining public trust and fostering ethical environmental stewardship. As we become increasingly dependent on AI for monitoring ecosystems, the underlying assumption that technology can provide all the answers may lead to complacency in human judgment and action. The challenge lies in balancing the immense possibilities offered by AI with a commitment to ethical practices that prioritize environmental justice and inclusivity in the decision-making process.

The Role of AI in Conservation Efforts

Innovative applications of AI are reshaping how conservation organizations approach the intricate challenges of wildlife protection and habitat preservation. By leveraging vast arrays of data, AI-driven systems can analyze patterns that were previously elusive to researchers and conservationists. Machine learning algorithms can process satellite imagery to identify deforestation and environmental degradation in real-time, allowing for immediate action to curb these threatening trends. This capability not only enhances the efficiency of monitoring programs but also assists in prioritizing areas for conservation efforts. AI tools facilitate the collection and analysis of data from various species, making it possible to predict their population dynamics and assess the viability of different conservation strategies. Engaging technology in this way offers a comprehensive means of understanding biodiversity and the factors that endanger it, thus empowering conservationists to devise informed, targeted interventions. The relevance of AI extends beyond mere data analysis; it plays a pivotal role in engaging communities and stakeholders in conservation initiatives. By utilizing AI-enabled platforms, organizations can raise awareness about environmental issues and promote proactive behaviors among local populations. Mobile applications that allow users to report wildlife sightings or illegal poaching activities not only facilitate data collection but also ignite community involvement in natural resource management. This fusion of technology and grassroots participation is crucial for sustaining long-term conservation efforts, as it fosters a sense of ownership and responsibility towards the environment. As local communities become active contributors to conservation data, AI systems can help streamline this information, amplifying the collective impact on policymaking. Integrating AI into public engagement strategies bridges the gap between science and society, making conservation a shared endeavor. As AI continues to evolve, ethical considerations regarding its application in conservation cannot be overlooked. The reliance on automated systems raises questions about the accuracy of data interpretation and the potential for bias in decision-making processes. Ensuring that AI tools are developed and deployed with a clear understanding of ecological complexities is essential for their successful integration into conservation strategies. Transparency in how AI algorithms function and the data they rely upon is critical to building trust among stakeholders, including indigenous populations whose knowledge is invaluable in these efforts. This highlights the need for multidisciplinary cooperation among technologists, ecologists, and local communities. By addressing these ethical dimensions, the conservation sector can harness the transformative potential of AI while safeguarding against unintended consequences that may arise from its use. As we navigate the intersection of AI and conservation, striking a balance between technological innovation and ethical responsibility becomes imperative for achieving sustainable outcomes.

XXI. THE FUTURE OF AI REGULATION

As technology continues to evolve at a staggering pace, the challenge of regulating AI has become increasingly complex. Policymakers must navigate a landscape characterized by rapid innovation and divergent interests from tech companies, governments, and civil society. While the potential benefits of AI, such as enhanced productivity and improved quality of life, are tempting, they come with significant ethical dilemmas regarding privacy, security, and job displacement. Striking a balance between fostering innovation and ensuring public safety is essential. This intricate dance necessitates a collaborative approach that includes stakeholders from technology, law, and the public sector to develop robust frameworks that can adapt to the swift shifts in AI capabilities. Without a unified regulatory strategy, the risk that unbridled advancements could exacerbate existing inequalities or lead to severe societal consequences looms large. Engaging with the ethical implications of AI regulation involves addressing issues including transparency, accountability, and bias. Regulators must establish clear guidelines that hold AI developers accountable for their technologies impacts. This means implementing standards for transparency that require companies to disclose how their algorithms function and the backgrounds of the datasets they utilize. Addressing bias in AI systems is crucial, as flawed algorithms can perpetuate discrimination and reinforce existing social inequities. As such, regulation should promote practices like independent audits and inclusive dataset collection methods, which ensure a more equitable representation within AI applications. By prioritizing ethical considerations in AI regulation, not only can harm be mitigated, but trust between the public and technology developers can also be bolstered, thus paving the way for a more responsible and socially conscious technological future. Looking ahead, the prospect of global collaboration in AI regulation could emerge as a pivotal mechanism for governing this transformative technology. With AI transcending national borders, international agreements and shared standards are essential for effective governance. Countries will need to engage in dialogues to establish guidelines that transcend local interests and address the global implications of AI. Fostering interdisciplinary research that includes technologists, ethicists, and social scientists can create a more comprehensive understanding of AIs broader societal impact. By adopting a multilateral approach to regulation, the global community can better manage the challenges posed by AI while harnessing its potential to improve human life. Emphasizing cooperation and shared responsibility will be key to navigating the uncharted waters of AI, laying the groundwork for a future that not only embraces innovation but also safeguards the principles of justice and equity for all.

Current Regulatory Frameworks

In navigating the complexities induced by rapid advancements in artificial intelligence, existing regulatory frameworks increasingly exhibit their limitations. Most current regulations were designed during a time when technology was static compared to today's dynamic landscape. Consequently, these frameworks often fail to account for the unique challenges posed by AI, such as accountability in decision-making processes and the ethical implications of algorithmic bias. Regulatory bodies are often unprepared for the pace at which innovation occurs; lengthy legislative processes can hinder the ability to implement timely measures to safeguard public interest effectively. This disconnect raises crucial questions about whether existing governance structures are adequate or if they require a complete overhaul to accommodate the unprecedented capabilities of AI technologies. The landscape of AI regulation is further complicated by the global nature of technological advancements. Many companies operate across international jurisdictions, making it challenging for any single nation to enforce regulations consistently. Inconsistent regulations can lead to a race to the bottom, where companies may relocate operations to regions with looser requirements, inadvertently exposing consumers to greater risks. Variations in data privacy laws, such as the General Data Protection Regulation (GDPR) in Europe and more lax frameworks in the United States, create an environment in which ethical considerations can easily be sidestepped. It is imperative for global entities and regulators to collaborate, establishing a cohesive and comprehensive approach to governance that recognizes the interconnected nature of technology and its far-reaching implications. Despite these challenges, there is a growing call for regulatory innovation that embraces a proactive rather than reactive approach to AI development. As awareness of AIs potential risks expands, regulatory initiatives are beginning to prioritize adaptive governance models that can evolve alongside technology. These models employ principles of transparency, accountability, and inclusivity in their frameworks, allowing stakeholders—ranging from governments to the public—to actively participate in shaping regulations. Such collaborative efforts could foster environments where technological advancement is harmonized with ethical considerations, ultimately leading to a more responsible approach to AI. Adopting these frameworks may serve not only to mitigate risks but also to encourage a sense of public trust in emerging technologies, allowing society to harness the benefits of AI while addressing ethical dilemmas as they arise.

The Need for International Standards

The rapid evolution of technologies, particularly in artificial intelligence, underscores the urgent need for universally recognized protocols and regulations. As AI systems increasingly influence critical areas such as healthcare, finance, and public safety, the absence of international standards can lead to disparate and often conflicting practices across nations. This situation not only complicates collaboration among countries but also creates unpredictable risks that could harm citizens or destabilize economies. Without agreed-upon ethical guidelines for AI deployment, malicious uses may emerge, undermining public trust and exacerbating social inequality. Establishing these standards can provide a framework through which nations can work collaboratively, sharing best practices and mitigating potential harms, ultimately facilitating a balanced approach to technological advancement. Navigating the complex landscape of AI can be particularly challenging due to its inherent capability to transcend borders. When technologies developed in one country proliferate globally without a cohesive regulatory framework, discrepancies in legislation can result in significant ethical dilemmas and operational inconsistencies. Such a scenario is evident in the development and deployment of facial recognition technologies, which may be embraced in some countries yet faced with resistance or stringent regulations in others. A unified set of international standards would encourage responsible innovation by providing clear guidelines for the acceptable use of AI, addressing issues such as privacy, consent, and accountability. Harmonizing these regulations would not only enhance safety and security but also foster an environment in which technological advancements serve as a force for good across various cultures and societies. Standardization holds the potential to level the playing field for nations at different stages of technological advancement. Developing countries often lack the resources and infrastructure to implement sophisticated AI systems effectively and ethically. By establishing international standards, these nations could access frameworks and support systems that promote equitable participation in the global technological arena. This inclusivity ensures that while leading nations drive AI innovation, emerging economies can adopt sustainable practices to harness these advancements responsibly. The establishment of international standards is not just a regulatory necessity, but a moral imperative, aimed at ensuring that the benefits of AI advancements are shared broadly, helping to create a more equitable future for all of humanity.

Balancing Innovation and Safety

In the rapidly evolving landscape of technology, the dichotomy between innovation and safety takes center stage. The pursuit of groundbreaking advancements often comes with the risk of unforeseen consequences that may jeopardize public well-being. The development of AI has the potential to streamline processes and enhance productivity across diverse sectors. Yet, the same technologies can inadvertently exacerbate existing social inequalities or lead to job displacement. As innovators push boundaries, it becomes essential for policymakers and stakeholders to establish robust frameworks that prioritize ethical considerations alongside technological development. This balancing act necessitates the collaboration of technologists, ethicists, and engineers, ensuring that innovations are not only advanced but are also aligned with societal values and safety protocols. Navigating the complexities of innovation introduces a myriad of ethical dilemmas that highlight the importance of precautionary measures. While the drive for technological progress can ignite a fervent sense of optimism about future possibilities, it also raises questions about accountability and oversight. Incidents such as biased algorithms in AI applications or the implications of privacy erosion illustrate the pressing need for regulatory frameworks that enforce standards and promote responsible innovation. Incorporating ethical practices into the design and deployment stages can mitigate potential risks, fostering public trust in new technologies. By establishing mechanisms for public input and employing interdisciplinary approaches, society can better harness technological breakthroughs while safeguarding against potential hazards, thus ensuring that progress does not come at the expense of safety and ethical integrity. The path forward involves an ongoing commitment to dialogue between innovation and safety standards. As AI technologies increasingly penetrate everyday life, fostering a culture of open communication among innovators, regulators, and the public is crucial. Educational initiatives aimed at raising awareness about AIs implications can empower individuals, equipping them with the knowledge to engage in meaningful discussions about its uses and abuses. Ongoing research into the socio-economic impacts of emerging technologies can guide policy decisions that are both prudent and progressive. As the world embraces new possibilities offered by advancements in AI, maintaining a vigilant and adaptable approach to safety will be paramount. In this way, society can strive not only for groundbreaking achievements but also for a technological future that prioritizes the well-being and ethical treatment of all individuals.

XXII. THE SINGULARITY AND HUMAN EVOLUTION

In the rapidly evolving landscape of technological advancement, the convergence of AI and human evolution is proving to be a transformative force. This intersection raises crucial questions about the direction in which humanity is headed, particularly as AI begins to augment cognitive abilities and physical capabilities. The potential for enhancements, whether through genetic modification or brain-computer interfaces, suggests a future where human capacities could surpass traditional biological limits. This not only opens doors to unprecedented opportunities for individuals and society as a whole but also leads to significant ethical dilemmas regarding the definition of what it means to be human. As we stand on the precipice of this new era, it becomes imperative to contemplate the implications of merging human intellect with machine learning and the potential societal shifts that could ensue. Similarly, the fear of technological singularity—a point at which AI surpasses human intelligence—heightens the stakes of this evolution. Should such a transformation occur, the fundamental balance of power and agency may shift dramatically. The existential risks associated with superintelligence cannot be understated, as machines possessing cognitive functions that exceed human reasoning might not necessarily align with human values or welfare. This scenario prompts urgent dialogue surrounding the governance of AI development and the necessity of ethical frameworks to guide its integration into society. Acknowledging the potential for both utopian enhancements and dystopian outcomes is essential for developing a balanced approach to these emerging technologies. Thus, an informed discourse regarding the risks and responsibilities of advanced AI will be critical in shaping a future where humans can coexist harmoniously with their creations. The prospect of human evolution in the context of the singularity extends beyond mere enhancement; it necessitates a reevaluation of identity, relationships, and societal structures. As humans integrate more deeply with technology, the nature of interpersonal connections may also evolve, potentially leading to new forms of community and interaction that blend the digital and physical realms. These changes could foster a more interconnected world but might also alienate individuals from traditional social frameworks. The challenge lies in navigating this duality—the opportunity for greater connectivity alongside the risk of isolation. As we advance toward the singularity, the dialogue surrounding human evolution must address not only the technological capabilities we are developing but also the profound implications these advancements hold for our collective psyche and social fabric. Thus, the intersection of the singularity and human evolution encapsulates a complex web of possibilities that demand ongoing scrutiny and ethical consideration.

Biological Enhancements Through AI

The integration of AI into biological enhancement presents an intriguing junction where technology meets human physiology. By leveraging AI, researchers are developing biologically compatible interfaces that could enhance human capabilities, from cognitive functions to physical attributes. The application of machine learning algorithms in genomics exemplifies this trend, as they facilitate the identification of genetic markers linked to specific traits. In doing so, AI not only allows for predictive analyses of health outcomes but also optimizes approaches in gene editing techniques like CRISPR. The implications of such enhancements are profound; with AI, it becomes conceivable to eradicate hereditary diseases or augment mental resilience, thus fundamentally altering our understanding of human potential and health. Yet, the allure of such enhancements raises critical ethical considerations that cannot be overlooked. As society embraces the possibility of AI-driven biological enhancements, issues surrounding equity and access amplify. The risk of perpetuating socio-economic divides is evident, as only a privileged faction may access these enhancements, potentially leading to a societal hierarchy based on biological capabilities. Ethical dilemmas surface regarding the manipulation of human genes and the essence of identity itself. Is enhancing cognitive abilities or physical performance merely an advancement in technology, or does it challenge the very definition of what it means to be human? Engaging in discussions about the ethical frameworks guiding such technologies becomes essential in navigating this complex landscape, ensuring that progress does not come at the expense of our moral compass. The future of humanity, intertwined with biological enhancements through AI, holds both promise and peril. As advancements in neurotechnology, prosthetics, and genetic modification escalate, they present unparalleled opportunities for overcoming disabilities and improving quality of life. These advancements also beckon caution regarding the potential for misuse and the unforeseen consequences of altering fundamental human traits. Exploring regulatory measures, such as oversight bodies that evaluate the implications of these technologies, becomes imperative. Balancing innovation with ethical responsibility is the pathway forward, ensuring that the quest for enhanced human abilities aligns with societal values and respects the intricate tapestry of human life. The journey through this transformative frontier calls for collective contemplation on the implications of our choices — shaping not just the future of technology but the essence of humanity itself.

The Concept of Post-Humanism

As we delve into the intricate interplay between human beings and technology, post-humanism emerges as a significant philosophical framework that challenges the traditional understanding of what it means to be human. Within this discourse, post-humanism questions the anthropocentric perspectives that have dominated Western thought for centuries. By emphasizing the fluidity of identity and the interdependence between humans and machines, this perspective opens up fertile ground for reevaluating ethical considerations and societal values. The acceleration of AI and biotechnological advancements creates an urgent need to rethink human agency, dignity, and the very essence of consciousness, as these technologies begin to alter human capacities and experiences. In doing so, post-humanism offers a lens through which we can critically engage with the implications of becoming more than human while recognizing our ontological ties to a broader ecosystem, which includes non-human entities. The implications of post-humanism extend beyond mere philosophical inquiry; they resonate deeply within practical fields such as ethics, art, and science. In bioethics, discussions surrounding genetic modification, cloning, and AI-infused medical practices challenge the parameters of moral responsibility and consent. Post-humanist thought provokes us to question the rights of newly created entities, whether they be advanced artificial intelligences or genetically enhanced humans. Similarly, in the realm of art and literature, post-humanism encourages new narratives that disrupt established notions of authorship and creativity, urging creators to explore collaborative relationships between humans and AI. These explorations not only reflect shifting paradigms in artistic production but also epitomize the post-human condition, where boundaries between creator and creation blur, ultimately reconfiguring our understanding of autonomy and legacy in a rapidly evolving landscape. The trajectory outlined by post-humanist philosophy has significant ramifications for the future of humanity as we forge ahead in an era characterized by unprecedented technological integration. Embracing a post-humanist framework necessitates a reconceptualization of progress, where the conventional metrics of human achievement are reevaluated in light of our interconnectedness with our creations. The integration of AI into everyday life calls for an awareness of how its capabilities might enhance human abilities while simultaneously raising existential questions about purpose and identity. As we stand on the precipice of a transformed existence, post-humanism emerges not merely as a theoretical proposition but as an essential compass guiding our ethical deliberations and practical actions in the realm of human-machine relations. Such an approach demands an inclusive dialogue that accommodates diverse perspectives, fostering a future where technology serves as a partner in the quest for meaning and understanding within an increasingly complex world.

Future Scenarios for Human Evolution

The trajectory of human evolution may increasingly intertwine with advancements in technology, particularly in AI (AI). As AI systems advance to levels where they can augment human cognitive and physical capabilities, we may witness a merging of biological and synthetic attributes. This hybridization raises profound questions about what it means to be human. Individuals may opt for neurological enhancements that improve memory retention or critical thinking, leading to a society where cognitive superiority becomes a commodity. Such developments could exacerbate existing inequalities, creating a bifurcated society of enhanced individuals versus those who remain unaugmented. The implications of these disparities on social cohesion and moral responsibility are significant, inviting debates on the ethical parameters surrounding genetic modification and cognitive enhancement. In contemplating future evolutionary scenarios, the likely rise of brain-computer interfaces (BCIs) stands out as a transformative development. These interfaces could allow direct communication between the human brain and machines, facilitating not only the exchange of information but also enhancing human sensory experiences. The potential for BCIs pushes the boundaries of traditional human capabilities, thereby redefining our interaction with the world. This raises critical concerns regarding privacy and agency; as minds become more interconnected with digital networks, the potential for data exploitation and manipulation escalates. The reliance on technology for cognitive functions could erode fundamental aspects of human experience, such as creativity and emotional intelligence, heightening the risk of losing integral elements of our humanity.

The ethical dilemmas surrounding the future of human evolution cannot be overlooked. As we navigate the possibilities of human enhancement through technological means, the moral implications of such choices become paramount. The fundamental question rests on whether we are willing to redefine what constitutes human identity in pursuit of improved quality of life. Key philosophical debates emerge around autonomy and informed consent, particularly regarding enhancements administered at a young age or through societal pressures. The dialogue around these topics must involve diverse global perspectives to ensure that advancements in AI and biotechnology benefit humanity as a whole and do not inadvertently reinforce systemic inequalities. Balancing innovation with ethical considerations will be essential as we forge new definitions of humanity in the face of an ever-accelerating technological landscape.

XXIII. THE ROLE OF CORPORATIONS IN AI DEVELOPMENT

Corporate entities serve as significant powerhouses in the arena of AI development, wielding resources, talent, and influence that can shape the trajectory of technological progress. These corporations leverage vast amounts of capital to create advanced AI systems, often outpacing public research initiatives. The concentrated resources allow for large-scale data collection, which is fundamental in training effective AI models. Corporations can attract top-tier talent through competitive compensation packages and advanced work environments, which fosters innovation. By maintaining proprietary technologies and platforms, these entities establish significant competitive advantages that can stifle smaller firms and limit public discourse on ethical AI usage. Consequently, while corporate involvement propels rapid advancements, it presents a challenge to creating a balanced ecosystem where diverse voices and initiatives can flourish alongside corporate interests. Market dynamics also compel corporations to prioritize efficiency and profitability over ethical considerations, leading to a range of moral dilemmas in AI development. Profit-driven motives can result in the deployment of systems that reinforce biases or compromise user privacy, creating societal repercussions that extend beyond mere market competition. In many cases, the push for rapid deployment of AI technologies, such as facial recognition or surveillance systems, disregards the potential consequences for marginalized populations. The lack of regulatory frameworks further exacerbates this issue, as corporations often operate in an environment with insufficient oversight, allowing them to prioritize short-term gains over long-term societal impact. Consequently, the need for a balanced approach is crucial, wherein ethical guidelines and regulatory measures keep pace with the rapid development of AI technologies, ensuring that corporate interests align with societal welfare and human rights. The future of AI development hinges on fostering collaborative relationships among corporations, academia, and governmental bodies to create a more equitable technological landscape. By encouraging partnerships that prioritize ethical standards and the open exchange of ideas, it is possible to harness the collective intelligence of diverse stakeholders. Universities and research institutions can provide invaluable insights and critiques of AI deployment, ensuring that developments are not solely profit-driven but also socially conscious. Corporations must be held accountable for the societal implications of their actions through transparent practices and responsible innovation. By cultivating a culture that values ethical considerations alongside competitive strategies, the potential for responsible AI adoption increases, ultimately leading to advancements that enhance human civilization rather than pose existential risks. This holistic approach can pave the way for a more just and equitable integration of AI technologies into society, amplifying their benefits while minimizing harm.

Corporate Responsibility in AI Ethics

In an era where AI systems are rapidly integrated into numerous sectors, the responsibility of corporations in guiding ethical AI practices has become paramount. Companies are no longer mere economic entities; they are increasingly viewed as moral agents capable of influencing societal norms and individual lives. As AI technologies evolve, organizations are tasked with establishing frameworks that mitigate risks and promote fairness, transparency, and accountability. Issues such as algorithmic bias and data privacy have surfaced as significant ethical concerns, necessitating proactive measures from corporations in both the development and deployment phases of AI systems. By implementing robust ethical guidelines, corporations can navigate these challenges, ensuring that their AI-driven solutions not only comply with regulations but also reinforce public trust in technology. Addressing ethical considerations in AI cannot be a superficial endeavor; it requires a fundamental cultural shift within organizations. Companies must foster an internal dialogue centered around ethical AI, involving cross-disciplinary teams that include technologists, ethicists, and stakeholders from diverse backgrounds. This collective approach encourages a holistic examination of potential impacts and ensures a wider range of perspectives on complex moral dilemmas. Regular training and resources dedicated to ethical AI practices can empower employees and leadership alike to recognize and address ethical quandaries that arise in AI integration. Establishing ethics boards or committees within corporations can provide oversight and encourage ongoing scrutiny of AI applications, fostering a commitment to responsible practices that go beyond mere compliance. Thus, building an ethical framework in AI not only safeguards against potential harm but also positions companies as leaders in the responsible development of transformative technology. A forward-thinking approach to corporate responsibility in AI ethics ultimately serves as a catalyst for innovation and societal benefit. By prioritizing ethical considerations, companies can differentiate themselves in a crowded marketplace, attracting consumers who value social responsibility alongside product effectiveness. Ethical AI practices can lead to the creation of more inclusive technologies that serve a broader demographic, addressing systemic issues rather than exacerbating them. An emphasis on transparency and moral accountability not only safeguards against legal repercussions but can also generate positive reputational benefits for the organization. As AI continues to shape the global landscape, the role of businesses in championing ethical standards will significantly influence not only their success but also the moral foundation of future technological advancements. Consequently, the pursuit of corporate responsibility in AI ethics is not merely an obligation; it is a profound opportunity for organizations to shape a future where technology enriches lives while upholding fundamental human values.

The Influence of Tech Giants

Amid growing discussions surrounding AI and its implications, the role of tech giants cannot be overlooked. Companies like Google, Amazon, and Microsoft are at the forefront of AI development, wielding immense influence over how technology is integrated into daily life. Their investments in machine learning and data analytics not only shape the landscape of technological advancement but also guide public perception and acceptance of AI. Through their substantial research and development budgets, these corporations solidify their status as pacesetters, often setting the standards that smaller firms strive to achieve. Their algorithms and platforms become ubiquitous, creating a cybersecurity feedback loop where the very frameworks meant to secure data can become instruments of control and surveillance. This duality makes their influence both transformative and potentially perilous, underscoring the necessity for oversight in the rapidly evolving tech space. While innovation remains a driving force for industry leaders, ethical considerations often take a backseat to profit and competitive advantage. Tech giants frequently prioritize rapid deployment of AI systems, enabling astonishing capabilities in automation and decision-making that could redefine industries. This speed often skims over the potential societal impacts of their technologies, such as job displacement and widening inequalities in access to information. As they maneuver within a relatively unregulated environment, questions arise concerning consumer privacy, data ownership, and algorithmic bias. Without a robust framework for accountability, significant risks emerge, suggesting that unchecked technological advancement might exacerbate social divides rather than assist in bridging them. In this light, the responsibility of these corporations extends beyond merely producing innovative technologies; it encompasses a broader obligation to ensure that the benefits of AI advancements are equitably distributed across diverse populations. The immense power tech companies wield also fosters a concerning dependency among users, instilling a culture of acceptance that can effectively render societal discourse on AI moot. As people integrate these technologies into their lives, ranging from virtual assistants to predictive analytics, an implicit trust builds around their reliability and ethical standards. This dependence raises alarms about the potential normalization of surveillance and control as users sacrifice privacy for convenience. This overwhelming influence cultivates a runaway cycle where the societal implications of AI are dictated less by democratic processes and more by corporate interests. Consequently, fostering greater public engagement becomes imperative to create an informed citizenry capable of navigating the complexities posed by advancing technologies. An active dialogue will not only help mitigate the unchecked influence of tech giants but will also ensure that AI's future development aligns with a broader ethical framework resilient to the exigencies of singularity.

Startups and Innovation in AI

The landscape of technology entrepreneurship is rapidly changing, driven largely by the relentless advancements in artificial intelligence. Startups are stepping into a pivotal role as they not only harness AIs transformative potential but also contribute significantly to its evolution. These entrepreneurial ventures often operate on the cutting edge of innovation, developing solutions that address unfulfilled needs across various sectors, from healthcare to finance. As these companies emerge, they stimulate competition and promote a culture of rapid iteration and refinement, allowing for the quick adaptation of AI technologies. The agility of startups compared to established firms enables them to experiment with novel business models and applications, thus acting as incubators for groundbreaking ideas that could redefine industry standards and societal norms. The symbiotic relationship between startups and AI innovation underscores a democratization of technology that was previously constrained by financial and institutional barriers. In an era where access to powerful AI tools and data is becoming increasingly available, entrepreneurs from diverse backgrounds can now build AI-driven solutions with significantly lower overheads. This newfound accessibility fosters a diverse ecosystem of innovations, where small teams can compete against larger, established corporations. The collaborative nature of the tech community, characterized by initiatives like open-source projects and shared knowledge platforms, enhances the speed and breadth of advancements in AI. Startups equipped with AI capabilities can swiftly iterate their products based on user feedback, leading to improved functionality and user satisfaction, which further fuels their growth and market impact. The rapid expansion of AI-focused startups raises critical questions about ethical considerations and societal implications. As these companies scale, the potential for misapplication of technology becomes more pronounced, including issues related to bias, privacy, and the displacement of jobs. It is crucial for entrepreneurs to be mindful of the societal context in which their innovations are deployed. Establishing ethical guidelines and promoting responsible AI practices is not merely a regulatory necessity but also a strategic advantage, as consumers increasingly demand transparency and accountability. Startups that prioritize ethical considerations in their development processes not only contribute to a more sustainable technological environment but also enhance their credibility and user trust. Thus, while startups are at the forefront of AI-driven innovation, they bear the responsibility of ensuring that their contributions to society are constructive, inclusive, and ethically sound, paving the way for a future that benefits all of humanity.

XXIV. PUBLIC ENGAGEMENT WITH AI

As societies grapple with the implications of AI, the role of public engagement becomes increasingly crucial in shaping these technologies development and deployment. Historically, advancements in technology have often outpaced the public's understanding and acceptance, leading to a disconnect between innovation and societal need. The introduction of AI into everyday life poses similar challenges; thus, fostering broader public discourse is essential for aligning these advancements with community values and expectations. This engagement can take various forms, including public forums, educational seminars, and interactive platforms, where individuals are encouraged to learn about AIs potential and limitations. By actively participating in conversations surrounding AI, the public can contribute to setting ethical standards and policy frameworks that ensure technology serves society rather than undermines it. The ways in which AI technologies are integrated into various sectors further highlight the need for informed public interaction. Industries such as healthcare, finance, and education are rapidly adopting AI solutions, often with limited transparency about their workings or the data they utilize. This lack of clarity can breed mistrust and anxiety among affected individuals. Public engagement is vital not only for educating people about how AI impacts their lives but also for empowering them to voice their concerns and influence decision-making processes. Public consultations on AI-related regulations can ensure that diverse perspectives are considered, fostering a sense of collective ownership over the technologies that are increasingly shaping human experiences. Meaningful involvement from the populace can lead to a more ethically robust integration of AI in various fields. While the promise of AI presents opportunities for transformative progress, it also poses significant ethical questions that demand public scrutiny and input. As these technologies evolve and their applications expand, the potential for biases and systemic inequities also grows. Issues such as data privacy, algorithmic bias, and the displacement of jobs are pertinent concerns that warrant active discussion and engagement from all societal sectors. Institutions, including governments and educational organizations, must prioritize establishing forums conducive to open dialogue about AIs roles and its implications. By creating a culture of transparency and inclusivity, stakeholders can collectively navigate the complexities of AI, striving towards solutions that mitigate risks while maximizing benefits. Engaging the public in these critical discussions ensures that AI's integration into society reflects a commitment to ethical principles and equity, ultimately fostering a future where technology enhances human well-being.

Raising Awareness and Understanding

In an era where AI threatens to reshape the very fabric of human existence, awareness and understanding become critical pre-conditions for navigating these profound changes. As individuals and societies grapple with the implications of AI, it is essential to foster a culture that promotes conversation about its nuances and complexities. This conversation should encompass not only the technological advancements themselves but also their ethical, social, and existential ramifications. By bringing diverse stakeholders into the dialogue—scientists, ethicists, policymakers, and community members—we create a multifaceted perspective that deepens our collective understanding of AI's impact. This interdisciplinary approach equips us to address questions and concerns, fostering a public discourse where informed opinions can flourish. Cultivating a well-informed society positions individuals to engage thoughtfully with AI developments, thus ensuring that technology serves humanity rather than undermining its core values. Understanding the implications of AI advancements goes beyond awareness; it necessitates active participation in shaping the future of its integration into society. Educational initiatives must be prioritized, emphasizing not only the functionalities of AI but also the ethical frameworks that govern its use. Programs that teach critical thinking and ethical reasoning in conjunction with technological literacy can empower individuals to interrogate the motivations behind AIs design and application. As potential users and beneficiaries of AI, individuals must be educated to recognize biases embedded in algorithms, data privacy concerns, and the societal implications of automating various sectors. By forging connections between theoretical knowledge and practical application, we foster a generation capable of approaching AI with both wonder and caution. Such empowerment is crucial for ensuring that future innovations align with humanistic values and serve as catalysts for positive societal change. Raising awareness and understanding concerning AI profoundly impacts the policymaking landscape. As technological advancements accelerate, lawmakers must be equipped with a robust grasp of AI's implications to craft informed regulations. Policy frameworks that emerge from informed discourse can facilitate responsible innovation, ensuring that advancements benefit society and mitigate potential risks. This involves not only establishing ethical guidelines but also fostering transparency and accountability in AI development. By prioritizing engagement with tech developers and ethicists, lawmakers can create a regulatory environment that incentivizes collaboration and ethical considerations. Public participation in the legislative process can engender trust between tech companies and the communities they affect. In this way, an informed populace not only holds policymakers accountable but also actively contributes to a system that embodies our shared aspirations for a thoughtful and just approach to AI integration.

Community Involvement in AI Discussions

Incorporating diverse voices into the discourse surrounding AI is essential for achieving a well-rounded understanding of its implications and potential. Community involvement not only fosters a more inclusive conversation but also ensures that the resulting technologies address the needs and concerns of various demographic groups. This integration of perspectives can help mitigate the risks of technological disparities, as marginalized communities often face different challenges than their more privileged counterparts. Engaging with diverse community stakeholders enables researchers and developers to anticipate and identify unintended consequences that may arise from their technologies, fostering a proactive rather than reactive approach to AI development. Educational initiatives play a critical role in facilitating community involvement in AI discussions. By providing accessible information and opportunities for engagement, educational programs can empower individuals from various backgrounds to participate meaningfully in the conversation. Workshops, forums, and public discussions can demystify complex concepts, making them more approachable for those who might not have a technical background. Encouraging curiosity about AI among the general populace helps to cultivate a critical awareness of its technologies, ultimately leading to a more informed citizenry that can advocate for ethical AI development. As communities become knowledgeable about the nuances of AI, they are better equipped to influence policy decisions, thereby holding developers and organizations accountable for the social and ethical ramifications of their innovations. To foster a sustainable culture of community involvement in AI discussions, it is crucial to establish ongoing dialogue between technologists and community representatives. This can be facilitated through partnerships with local organizations, fostering relationships that go beyond one-time consultations. Adequate representation in AI-related initiatives ensures that the voices of those often overlooked in technological advancements are heard and considered. Feedback loops that allow communities to share their experiences with AI technologies can further enhance this relationship, providing developers with invaluable insights that inform their work. By creating a collaborative environment in which all stakeholders feel valued and heard, the field of AI can evolve responsibly and ethically, ultimately serving humanity in a way that reflects our collective values and priorities.

The Role of Media in Shaping AI Narratives

In contemporary discourse, the portrayal of AI often takes center stage within various media outlets, shaping public perception and understanding. The manner in which AI is depicted—whether as a threatening force or a transformative tool—carries significant implications for societal reactions and policies. Sensationalized narratives, often characterized by dystopian themes in films and news articles, can evoke widespread fear regarding the potential dangers of AI, including job displacement and loss of control. This sensationalism may lead to a public outcry for regulation and ethical considerations that might stifle innovation. Conversely, media representations that highlight AIs beneficial applications, such as in healthcare or education, can foster a sense of optimism and acceptance, thus encouraging collaborative efforts to harness its potential while addressing ethical concerns. The narratives constructed by media not only inform but also influence the trajectory of AI development and its acceptance within society. The role of social media further complicates the landscape of AI narratives by allowing diverse voices to contribute to the discourse, often outside traditional journalism. Platforms like Twitter and Reddit serve as battlegrounds for competing ideologies surrounding AI, where grassroots movements can both support and challenge prevailing narratives disseminated by mainstream media. This democratization of information enables individuals to engage with AI on a personal level, sharing their experiences and apprehensions. Yet, the fragmentation of opinions can lead to misinformation and polarization, reinforcing biases rather than fostering informed discussions. Influential figures or organizations can shape public understanding by amplifying certain perspectives, creating echo chambers that either vilify or glorify AI technologies. This dynamic interplay exemplifies how user-generated content can both enrich and distort the dialogue around AI, ultimately affecting regulatory decisions, funding allocations, and behavioral shifts within society. As AI continues to evolve, the responsibility of media in shaping its narratives cannot be overstated. Ethical considerations come into play when media outlets decide which stories to amplify, reflecting broader societal values and concerns. A balanced portrayal that includes not only the potential benefits but also the attendant risks of AI can help prepare society for the ramifications of this technology. Education plays a critical role, as media literacy can empower the public to discern factual information from sensationalized claims. It is essential for both media producers and consumers to engage critically with AI narratives to create a more nuanced understanding of its implications. The way AI is framed in media will significantly impact not just policies and regulations but also the cultural narratives that define how humanity interacts with this transformative technology, guiding it towards a future that aligns with our collective ethical and existential values.

XXV. PREPARING FOR THE SINGULARITY

As we stand on the precipice of unprecedented technological advancement, the landscape of human existence is set to undergo transformative changes that require thoughtful preparation. Central to this transition is the concept of the Singularity, a term that encapsulates the moment when AI surpasses human intelligence, leading to rapid, unforeseeable advancements. Preparing effectively for this shift entails not only advancements in technology and science but also the cultivation of a societal framework capable of embracing such changes. This involves interdisciplinary collaboration that blends ethics, philosophy, and policy-making alongside the advancements in AI. By proactively addressing these various dimensions, society can ensure that innovations are aligned with human values and contribute positively to the collective good. Ethical considerations must form the backbone of our preparation for the Singularity, as the potential risks associated with unfettered AI development cannot be overstated. As advancements in AI become increasingly autonomous, concerns about decision-making authority, accountability, and the ramifications of such technologies on employment are exacerbated. Addressing these issues necessitates robust discussions around the moral implications of AI systems. Who is responsible when an AI system makes a harmful decision? While the pursuit of technological capability is often viewed through a lens of progress, it is imperative to integrate ethical frameworks that prioritize human welfare and global equity. Advocacy for transparency, fairness, and inclusivity in AI design can foster public trust and facilitate a smoother transition towards a future profoundly influenced by these innovations. Engaging with educational initiatives is another critical aspect of preparing for the Singularity. As advancements in AI forge ahead, there is a pressing need for educational systems to adapt and equip individuals with the necessary skills to thrive in this changing environment. Emphasizing critical thinking, creativity, and interdisciplinary knowledge will prepare future generations to navigate increasingly complex technological landscapes. Public awareness campaigns can demystify AI, fostering a more comprehensive understanding among the broader population regarding its implications and potential. By actively encouraging interdisciplinary studies encompassing AI, ethics, sociology, and technology, society can cultivate a more informed citizenry that is not only adept at understanding these complex innovations but also engaged in shaping their trajectory for the benefit of all. Such concerted efforts will lay the groundwork for a future where humanity can harmoniously coexist with the machines it creates.

Strategies for Individuals and Societies

The advent of AI presents unique opportunities and formidable challenges for both individuals and societies. At the individual level, embracing lifelong learning is essential in adapting to a rapidly evolving job market shaped by AI advancements. Continuous education and skill upgrading enable individuals to remain relevant and proficient in emerging technologies, fostering resilience against obsolescence. By focusing on adaptability, people can harness the potential of AI as a collaborative partner rather than viewing it as a competitor. Developing soft skills such as creativity, emotional intelligence, and critical thinking will be paramount, as these are areas where human capabilities continue to outshine machines. Individuals who proactively engage with these strategies will not only secure their own futures but also contribute to a more innovative and flexible workforce, ready to tackle the demands of an AI-driven world. A cohesive societal strategy must also be established to address the ethical implications of AI technologies. Policymakers play a crucial role in creating regulatory frameworks that ensure AI systems promote equity, transparency, and accountability. It is imperative for leaders to engage diverse stakeholders, including technologists, ethicists, and community members, in conversations about the direction of AI development. Establishing ethical guidelines and standards that prevent biases in AI algorithms will be essential to safeguard marginalized groups. Integrating AI literacy into educational curricula can empower future generations to critically evaluate AIs role in society, fostering informed citizens who can advocate for responsible AI use. Through collaborative dialogue and proactive governance, societies can cultivate a shared understanding of AI, allowing them to beneficially incorporate these technologies while minimizing the risks associated with their deployment. Fostering a culture of innovation emerges as a critical strategy for both individuals and societies in the face of impending singularity. Encouraging environments that support experimentation and entrepreneurship can spur technological breakthroughs and enhance societal well-being. By investing in research and development, governments and private sectors can create incubator programs that facilitate the growth of startups focused on sustainable AI applications. Supporting interdisciplinary partnerships can lead to novel solutions that address complex social challenges—ranging from healthcare to environmental sustainability. Cultivating an atmosphere that embraces risk-taking, alongside a robust support system, allows individuals to explore unconventional ideas that could unlock transformative potential. Consequently, as societies navigate the intersection of humanity and advanced technologies, they must prioritize a creative ethos that harnesses the power of AI to drive positive change, ultimately enriching the human experience.

The Importance of Interdisciplinary Approaches

As the boundaries between disciplines continue to blur, the significance of an interdisciplinary approach becomes increasingly evident in addressing the multifaceted challenges posed by AI and its repercussions on human society. Expert insights drawn from fields such as ethics, cognitive science, engineering, sociology, and environmental studies foster a rich tapestry of understanding that cannot be achieved through a singular lens. The ethical implications of AI systems designed for decision-making directly intersect with psychology, necessitating a comprehensive analysis of human behavior as it interacts with these technologies. Capturing the intricacies inherent in this relationship not only enhances our comprehension of the ethical dilemmas but also underscores the urgent need for frameworks that consider diverse perspectives, ultimately leading to innovative solutions that prioritize humanity amid rapid technological advancement. Collaboration across disciplines can yield insights that are crucial in navigating the unpredictable landscape shaped by AI. Advancements in AI hold the promise of innovations in healthcare, yet the implementation of these technologies must be scrutinized through a sociological lens to account for disparities in access and impact. The importance of cross-sector partnerships among researchers, healthcare professionals, and policymakers cannot be overstated. By examining case studies where interdisciplinary approaches successfully addressed health equity issues, we can highlight the potential to create more inclusive AI systems that are sensitive to diverse populations. Engaging varied expertise allows for a thorough vetting of the potential societal implications resulting from AI integration, illuminating pathways toward equitable improvement in quality of life across different communities. This fusion of knowledge not only leads to more robust technological advancements but also fosters a more just society. The significance of interdisciplinary engagement extends to addressing the ethical quandaries that surface with AIs evolution. In exploring the advancements in AI technologies such as machine learning and predictive algorithms, ethical considerations must be rooted in philosophical inquiry to frame discussions around autonomy, privacy, and accountability. Interdisciplinary dialogue enables a more holistic grasp of the paradoxes introduced by intelligent systems, as input from legal experts can elucidate regulatory frameworks that balance innovation with protection. This integrated approach encourages a culture of responsibility within the tech industry while fostering transparency and trust among stakeholders. By transcending conventional barriers, we can cultivate an environment where innovation serves humanity's best interests, aligning technological progress with ethical standards and leading to a more comprehensive understanding of the human-AI relationship in our rapidly evolving world.

Fostering Resilience in the Face of Change

In the rapidly evolving landscape of technological advancement, the capacity to adapt becomes a crucial asset for individuals and societies alike. Amidst the uncertainties brought about by pervasive changes in AI and other emerging technologies, resilience emerges as a vital quality that can enable individuals to navigate these shifts more effectively. Resilience is not merely the ability to endure challenges; it reflects a dynamic process of growth and adaptation in response to changing circumstances. By fostering a mindset that embraces flexibility and perseverance, individuals can better manage stress and mitigate the potential negative impacts of rapid change. This adaptive capacity facilitates not only personal growth but also enhances the collective ability of communities to respond to innovative disruptions in their socio-economic environments. Fostering resilience is intricately tied to the development of critical thinking skills and emotional intelligence. As individuals encounter complex scenarios that AI technologies can present, cultivating an awareness of one's own emotional responses and cognitive biases becomes essential. Critical thinking allows individuals to assess the implications of technological change, enabling them to make informed decisions amid uncertainty. Emphasizing education that prioritizes problem-solving skills—not just rote memorization—can empower learners to face the unpredictable landscape brought on by innovations. Emotional intelligence, which encompasses self-regulation and empathy, aids individuals in maintaining interpersonal relationships and collaborative networks that can serve as a support system during challenging transitions. By integrating these competencies into educational frameworks and professional training, societies reinforce resilience, preparing people to thrive in an ever-evolving technological world. Resilience in the face of change is a multifaceted endeavor that influences not only individual well-being but also societal cohesion. A community that actively promotes adaptability and mutual support fosters an environment where innovation can flourish without undermining social stability. Engagement through dialogue and shared experiences is essential for building resilient communities capable of responding to the complexities introduced by AI and other technologies. In this context, policymakers, educators, and community leaders share a responsibility to cultivate spaces where adaptability is valued, and diverse perspectives are heard. By investing in resource networks that encourage civic engagement, skill acquisition, and emotional support, societies can safeguard against the destabilizing effects of transformation. In doing so, they ensure that the benefits of technological progress can be enjoyed by all, paving the way for a more equitable future that embraces change as an opportunity for collective growth.

XXVI. CONCLUSION

The exploration of AI and its implications for humanity extends beyond mere technological advancements. Historically, revolutions in technology have prompted profound changes in societal structures, culture, and human experience. The potential for transforming human life remains intertwined with both the hope for a more efficient, equitable future and the cautionary tales of ethical dilemmas that these technologies may promote. Understanding the balance between innovation and responsibility is crucial. As we stand on the precipice of the singularity, it is essential to ask not only what we can achieve with AI, but also what we ought to pursue in our collective moral landscape. This duality highlights the need for continuous dialogue among scientists, ethicists, policymakers, and the general public to navigate these complex waters. Emerging technologies, particularly artificial intelligence, promise to redefine every facet of our existence—from healthcare and education to privacy and employment. The author's investigation into the exponential growth of these fields provides ample evidence of their potential to solve some of the most pressing challenges facing society today. Such advancements also risk exacerbating existing inequalities and creating new societal divides. It is imperative to formulate guidelines and frameworks that ensure equitable access to technology while safeguarding individual rights and freedoms. Engaging with these challenges is not merely an academic exercise but a moral obligation, as the trajectory of our civilization hinges on decisions made today regarding the deployment and regulation of these transformative technologies. The future of humanity in the age of AI rests in our hands, prompting an urgent need for proactive engagement. While the prospect of a technologically advanced civilization is enticing, it is accompanied by significant ethical considerations that demand our attention. The concerns surrounding AI—ranging from decision-making biases to questions of autonomy—illustrate the importance of fostering an interdisciplinary approach to innovation. As we venture forward, it is essential to cultivate a mindset where technological progress is guided by a deep-rooted ethical framework. Embracing this perspective not only prepares us for the challenges of tomorrow but also ensures that our transformation remains genuinely human-focused, benefiting individuals and societies as a whole.

Summary of Key Insights

Advancements in AI are reshaping the landscape of human existence, suggesting a pivotal moment in history where technology and humanity converge. This convergence signals an unprecedented shift in how we engage with our environment, work,
and even with each other. The exponential growth of technologies such as nanoscience and biotechnology complements AIs
evolution, creating new opportunities and capabilities. While
these innovations promise enhanced efficiency and capabilities,
they also raise critical questions regarding sustainability, equity,
and the intrinsic nature of human identity. As we navigate these
changes, it becomes increasingly important to critically analyze
both the potential benefits and the challenges they present to
society. Engaging with these insights fosters a deeper understanding of the dual-edged sword that AI represents and sets
the stage for ethical deliberations about the future trajectory of
human evolution. A central concern in discussions about AI is its
ethical implications, which cannot be underestimated. Emerging
technologies have the power to redefine not only practical aspects of life, such as employment and education, but also philosophical inquiries surrounding autonomy, free will, and social
responsibility. The potential for AI to outperform humans in various tasks raises concerns about obsolescence and the displacement of the workforce. There are questions about the moral status of AI entities and their role in decision-making processes
that directly affect human lives. Throughout the exploration of
these issues, it is vital to adopt a multidisciplinary approach
that combines insights from technology, ethics, sociology, and

philosophy, thereby enriching our understanding of how to navigate AIs integration into society. Establishing robust ethical frameworks will be pivotal in ensuring that the adoption of AI serves the common good rather than exacerbating existing inequalities. In grappling with the rapid evolution of AI, it becomes evident that the relationship between technology and humanity is not merely transactional; rather, it is transformative. As human beings enhance their capabilities through AI, they simultaneously confront questions of purpose and existence that challenge pre-existing notions of what it means to be human. The book highlights that these transformations could lead to an improved civilization armed with intelligent systems capable of addressing complex societal issues. Still, it also serves as a cautionary tale about the existential risks that come with unregulated advancements. A balanced consideration of the promises and perils of AI is crucial as we step into this new frontier. Embracing a forward-thinking perspective will enable society to harness the potential of AI responsibly, fostering an environment where technological innovation promotes ethical progress and a more inclusive future for all.

The Importance of Ethical Considerations

In the context of rapid advancements in artificial intelligence, understanding the implications of these technologies becomes increasingly crucial. The ethical considerations surrounding AI development extend beyond mere regulatory compliance; they encompass moral responsibilities to society. As algorithms make decisions that can affect significant aspects of everyday life—ranging from healthcare to criminal justice—the principles guiding their creation and implementation must ensure fairness, accountability, and transparency. Without a robust ethical framework, there is a risk of exacerbating existing societal inequalities, as biased algorithms could further marginalize vulnerable populations. Thus, proactively addressing ethical concerns is not merely an optional aspect of AI development; it is a necessity that can shape the trajectory of technological innovation and its integration into the fabric of human society. Ethical considerations influence public perception and acceptance of emerging technologies. As AI systems increasingly permeate various sectors, the trust of the public becomes paramount. Concerns about data privacy, surveillance, and decision-making processes can lead to widespread skepticism or resistance. When corporations and developers prioritize ethical guidelines, they can build transparent models that not only enhance user trust but also encourage broader societal acceptance of AI innovations. This journey toward ethical accountability fosters an environment where technology can be perceived as a partner in progress rather than a threat. As technological complexity grows, so does the necessity to engage diverse stakeholders in discussions about the potential risks and benefits, further underscoring the need for ethical deliberation in AI advancements. The incorporation of ethical considerations is fundamental for fostering responsible innovation during the era of the singularity. As humanity stands on the precipice of potentially transformative technological breakthroughs, it is essential to recognize that the choices made today will reverberate through time. By embedding ethical reflections into the design, development, and deployment of AI systems, creators can ensure that these technologies align with human values and enhance the quality of life rather than detract from it. Interdisciplinary collaboration among ethicists, technologists, policymakers, and the public will be vital in crafting comprehensive frameworks that guide even the most advanced AI systems. Prioritizing ethics in AI development not only safeguards humanity's interests but also paves a clearer path toward a future where technology and human values coalesce harmoniously.

Future Directions for Research and Policy

Looking ahead, it becomes imperative to consider how interdisciplinary collaboration can pave the way for more comprehensive research and policies regarding artificial intelligences rapid evolution. Traditionally, advancements in AI have been approached from a technical standpoint, often isolating their implications from societal and ethical considerations. Moving forward, researchers should adopt a more holistic methodology that incorporates perspectives from sociology, psychology, and other relevant fields. This integration will not only enhance our understanding of AIs multifaceted impacts but also inform policy frameworks that are both innovative and socially responsible. Involving diverse stakeholders, including ethicists, technologists, and community leaders, in the research process can result in a rich dialogue that addresses potential consequences before they manifest. Establishing platforms for continuous engagement will ensure that policy development remains adaptive and forward-looking, ultimately leading to a more balanced technological integration in society. Another significant area of focus for future policy development is the ethical regulation of emerging AI technologies. As AI systems become increasingly sophisticated, questions concerning decision-making, accountability, and transparency arise, necessitating robust frameworks that govern these technologies responsibly. Policymakers must prioritize the formulation of guidelines that address the ethical deployment of AI, taking cues from existing ethical codes in medical science and data privacy. International cooperation will be paramount in this endeavor, as the borderless nature of technology outpaces national regulations. Adopting a proactive stance towards global standards can facilitate a collaborative approach to addressing shared challenges, ensuring that AI advancements are aligned with human values. This involves not only risk management but also ethical training for developers and users, establishing a culture of accountability throughout the AI lifecycle. Prioritizing ethical standards in AI will safeguard both individual rights and societal wellbeing. Environmental sustainability also warrants serious consideration as we chart the future of AI research and policy. The integration of AI in various sectors can contribute to addressing pressing environmental issues, from optimizing energy use in urban settings to enhancing agricultural efficiency. The environmental footprint of AI technologies, particularly in data storage and processing, raises concerns about their long-term sustainability. Future research agendas must prioritize the development of green AI initiatives that focus on minimizing resource consumption and reducing waste in AI operations. Policies should incentivize the adoption of energy-efficient technologies and renewable resources in AI infrastructure. Integrating environmental impact assessments into AI project proposals can ensure that ecological considerations are inherent in the decision-making process. Prioritizing sustainability in AI development will not only mitigate negative environmental consequences but also promote a vision of technological advancement that harmonizes with the planets ecological limits.

Final Thoughts on Human Transformation Through AI

Technological integration into daily life has irrevocably altered human interactions, cognition, and even emotional responses. As AI becomes increasingly entrenched in various aspects of society—from social media algorithms influencing our worldviews to AI-driven healthcare systems enhancing patient outcomes—its capacity to reshape human experience is undeniable. This transformation suggests that the boundaries of identity and personal agency are becoming more fluid, prompting critical reflections on how individuals perceive themselves in relation to AI. The implications of this metamorphosis can be both enlightening and daunting. While some may find empowerment in utilizing AI tools to enhance creativity and productivity, others might experience alienation, leading to existential questions regarding autonomy and purpose in a world where machines play an often dominant role. The relationship between AI and humanity raises pressing ethical considerations around equity, accountability, and the digital divide. As technology progresses at a pace that often outstrips regulatory frameworks, the disparities between those who have access to these innovations and those who do not can widen significantly. This gap is more than a mere issue of access; it encompasses cultural shifts in how society defines success, emotional intelligence, and interpersonal relationships. As AI systems gain the ability to analyze emotional states and predict behavior, there is a risk of commodifying human experience. The cultivation of social skills and emotional awareness may be sidelined as people increasingly rely on AI for social interactions, posing profound implications for community cohesion and individual well-being. In this context, the transformation spurred by AI is not just technological, but also deeply sociocultural. In contemplating the efficacy of human transformation through AI, one must consider the dual-edged sword of progress. On one hand, emerging technologies hold the promise of unprecedented advancements in communication, productivity, and well-being, potentially catalyzing a new era of human flourishing. The ethical dilemmas posed by AIs growing influence demand a cautious approach to its integration into society. Engaging with these technologies necessitates a proactive dialogue about their implications, as well as an examination of our shared values and objectives as a civilization. The pathway to a positive future hinges on our ability to navigate this transformation thoughtfully, balancing innovation with a robust ethical framework that prioritizes human dignity and agency. In this new landscape, the trajectory of human identity will be a collaborative effort, founded on principles that honor the complexities of both technology and humanity.

BIBLIOGRAPHY

Minghai Zheng. 'How to Foster Resilience in Times of Change and Uncertainty in the Workplace.' Amazon Digital Services LLC - Kdp, 7/20/2023

Pam Grossman. 'Interdisciplinary Curriculum.' Challenges to Implementation, Sam Wineburg, Teachers College Press, 9/8/2000

Rodolphe Durand. 'Organizations, Strategy and Society.' The Orgology of Disorganized Worlds, Routledge, 11/27/2014

Benjamin Eli Smith. 'The Century Dictionary and Cyclopedia: The Century dictionary ... prepared under the superintendence of William Dwight Whitney.' William Dwight Whitney, Century Company, 1/1/1903

Kanta Dihal. 'AI Narratives.' A History of Imaginative Thinking about Intelligent Machines, Stephen Cave, Oxford University Press, 2/28/2020

William B. Weeks. 'AI for Good.' Applications in Sustainability, Humanitarian Action, and Health, Juan M. Lavista Ferres, John Wiley & Sons, 1/23/2024

Dean Burnett. 'Psycho-Logical.' Why Mental Health Goes Wrong – and How to Make Sense of It, Faber & Faber, 2/2/2021

Xerxes Minocher. 'Articulating AI.' From Private Power to Public Engagement, ProQuest LLC, 1/1/2023

Lomit Patel. 'Lean AI.' How Innovative Startups Use AI to Grow, "O'Reilly Media, Inc.", 1/30/2020

Jack Lasky. 'The Impact of the Tech Giants.' Greenhaven Press, a part of Gale, Cengage Learning, 1/1/2016

Reinhard Altenburger. 'Responsible Artificial Intelligence.' Challenges for Sustainable Management, René Schmidpeter, Springer Nature, 2/1/2023

Joshua Gans. 'The Economics of Artificial Intelligence.' Health Care Challenges, Ajay Agrawal, University of Chicago Press, 3/14/2024

Sergio Rijo. 'Post-Human Evolution.' Merging with Technology for Enhanced Consciousness, SERGIO RIJO, 1/16/2024

Cary Wolfe. 'What Is Posthumanism?.' U of Minnesota Press, 11/30/2013

Tracy J. Trothen. 'Religion and the Technological Future.' An Introduction to Biohacking, Artificial Intelligence, and Transhumanism, Calvin Mercer, Springer Nature, 2/22/2021

Ray Kurzweil. 'The Singularity is Near.' When Humans Transcend Biology, Penguin Books, 1/1/2006

Lisa Bodell. 'Balancing Innovation and Risk.' LinkedIn, 1/1/2020

Charles B. Phucas. 'Symposium on International Standards Information and ISONET.' Proceedings of a Symposium Held at the National Bureau of Standards, Gaithersburg, Maryland, October 11-12, 1979, U.S. Department of Commerce, National Bureau of Standards, 1/1/1980

Robert Haffner. 'Do Current Regulatory Frameworks in the EU Support Innovation and Security of Supply in Electricity and Gas Infrastructure?.' Final Report, Publications Office of the European Union, 1/1/2019

Mark Fenwick. 'Robotics, AI and the Future of Law.' Marcelo Corrales, Springer, 11/2/2018

Milind Tambe. 'AI and Conservation.' Fei Fang, Cambridge University Press, 3/28/2019

Zhou, Jun. 'Computer Vision and Pattern Recognition in Environmental Informatics.' IGI Global, 10/19/2015

Mohamed Ahmed Alloghani. 'AI and Sustainability.' Springer Nature, 11/25/2023

Benedetta Brevini. 'Is AI Good for the Planet?.' John Wiley & Sons, 10/14/2021

National Academy of Engineering. 'Examining Core Elements of International Research Collaboration.' Summary of a Workshop, Institute of Medicine, National Academies Press, 9/29/2011

Ryan Sullivan (Army officer). 'The U.S., China, and AI Competition Factors.' China Aerospace Studies Institute, 1/1/2021

Fatima Roumate. 'AI and the New World Order.' New weapons, New Wars and a New Balance of Power, Springer Nature Switzerland, 5/9/2024

Marcello Ienca. 'AI in Brain and Mental Health: Philosophical, Ethical & Policy Issues.' Fabrice Jotterand, Springer Nature, 2/11/2022

David D. Luxton. 'AI in Behavioral and Mental Health Care.' Academic Press, 9/10/2015

Eric Topol. 'Deep Medicine.' How AI Can Make Healthcare Human Again, Basic Books, 3/12/2019

StoryBuddiesPlay. 'Ideogram AI for Artists.' Exploring New Art Forms with Ideogram AI, StoryBuddiesPlay, 5/29/2024

Roger B. Dannenberg. 'Music and AI.' Alexandra Bonnici, Frontiers Media SA, 3/16/2021

York P. Herpers. 'The Art And The Artificial Intelligence: How The Value Of Real Art Is Increased.' Herpers Publishing Int, 8/5/2023

Alexander Manu. 'Transcending Imagination.' AI and the Future of Creativity, CRC Press, 4/19/2024

Holmes, Wayne. 'AI and education.' A guidance for policymakers, Miao, Fengchun, UNESCO Publishing, 4/8/2021

Julia V. Clark. 'STEM Education in Underserved Schools.' Promoting Equity, Access, and Excellence, JHU Press, 11/14/2023

UNESCO International Centre for Technical and Vocational Education and Training. 'Understanding the impact of AI on skills development.' UNESCO Publishing, 4/2/2021

Jac Ka Lok Leung. 'AI Literacy in K-16 Classrooms.' Davy Tsz Kit Ng, Springer Nature, 12/7/2022

Chemmalar S. 'AI and Global Strategic Trends.' Eliva Press, 2/17/2021

Paul Carroll. 'Billion Dollar Lessons.' What You Can Learn from the Most Inexcusable Business Failures of the Last Twenty-five Years, Portfolio, 1/1/2008

Dmitry Shargorodsky. 'Microsoft Dynamics 365 AI for Business Insights.' Transform your business processes with the practical implementation of Dynamics 365 AI modules, Packt Publishing Ltd, 3/29/2024

Daniel Hedblom. 'AI for Arts.' Niklas Hageback, CRC Press, 8/24/2021

Hugo Neri. 'The Risk Perception of Artificial Intelligence.' Rowman & Littlefield, 12/16/2020

Marcel Danesi. 'AI-Generated Popular Culture.' A Semiotic Perspective, Springer Nature, 1/1/2024

Malik Ghallab. 'Reflections on AI for Humanity.' Bertrand Braunschweig, Springer Nature, 2/6/2021

Simon Atuah Asakipaam. 'AI Ethics in Higher Education: Insights from Africa and Beyond.' Caitlin C. Corrigan, Springer Nature, 1/20/2023

Lauren B. Resnick. 'The Nature of Intelligence.' Lawrence Erlbaum Associates, 1/1/1976

Pentti O Haikonen. 'Consciousness And Robot Sentience (Second Edition).' World Scientific, 5/23/2019

Chris Fields. 'Great Philosophical Objections to Artificial Intelligence.' The History and Legacy of the AI Wars, Eric Dietrich, Bloomsbury Publishing, 1/14/2021

Duncan MacIntosh. 'Lethal Autonomous Weapons.' Re-Examining the Law and Ethics of Robotic Warfare, Jai Galliott, Oxford University Press, 1/19/2021

Fouad Sabry. 'Global Catastrophic Risk.' Fundamentals and Applications, One Billion Knowledgeable, 7/2/2023

Mr. Ghiath Shabsigh. 'Powering the Digital Economy: Opportunities and Risks of AI in Finance.' El Bachir Boukherouaa, International Monetary Fund, 10/22/2021

Frank Pasquale. 'Oxford Handbook of Ethics of AI.' Markus D. Dubber, Oxford University Press, 6/30/2020

Marion Real. 'Co-creation for Responsible Research and Innovation.' Experimenting with Design Methods and Tools, Alessandro Deserti, Springer Nature, 9/16/2021

Isabel Pedersen. 'Augmentation Technologies and AI in Technical Communication.' Designing Ethical Futures, Ann Hill Duin, Taylor & Francis, 6/1/2023

Emmy Wealth. 'Human-AI Collaboration.' The Future of Work, Blurb, Incorporated, 1/18/2024

Alpaslan Özerdem. 'Managing Emergencies and Crises.' Naim Kapucu, Jones & Bartlett Publishers, 10/13/2011

Abhishek Kumar. 'Visualization Techniques for Climate Change with Machine Learning and Artificial Intelligence.' Ashutosh Kumar Dubey, Elsevier, 11/11/2022

Sunil Mathew. 'Sustainability and Global Challenges.' Analysis by Mathematics of Uncertainty, John N. Mordeson, Springer Nature, 1/1/2024

Andrew Imbrie. 'The New Fire.' War, Peace, and Democracy in the Age of AI, Ben Buchanan, MIT Press, 3/8/2022

Board on Population Health and Public Health Practice. 'A Nationwide Framework for Surveillance of Cardiovascular and Chronic Lung Diseases.' Institute of Medicine, National Academies Press, 8/26/2011

Rony Medaglia. 'Research Handbook on Public Management and Artificial Intelligence.' Yannis Charalabidis, Edward Elgar Publishing, 1/1/2024

Daniel D. Lee. 'The AI State: Governing in the Age of Disruption and Rapid Technological Change.' SkyCuration, 5/3/2024

Glen A. Mazis. 'Humans, Animals, Machines.' Blurring Boundaries, SUNY Press, 9/4/2008

Susan B. Levin. 'Posthuman Bliss?.' The Failed Promise of Transhumanism, Oxford University Press, 1/1/2020

Shah Rukh. 'Masters of Tomorrow.' Redefining Human Potential with Future Technology, Amazon Digital Services LLC - Kdp, 10/16/2023

Eric Schmidt. 'The Age of AI.' And Our Human Future, Henry Kissinger, John Murray, 1/1/2021

William Welser IV. 'An Intelligence in Our Image.' The Risks of Bias and Errors in Artificial Intelligence, Osonde A. Osoba, Rand Corporation, 4/5/2017

Gupta, Brij B.. 'Security, Privacy, and Forensics Issues in Big Data.' Joshi, Ramesh C., IGI Global, 8/30/2019

Muzaffar Munshi. 'The Ethics Of Artificial Intelligence: Balancing Benefits and Risks.' Muzaffar Munshi, 5/13/2023

National Research Council. 'Ethical Considerations for Research on Housing-Related Health Hazards Involving Children.' Institute of Medicine, National Academies Press, 11/10/2005

David A. Mindell. 'The Work of the Future.' Building Better Jobs in an Age of Intelligent Machines, David H. Autor, MIT Press, 6/21/2022

B. Carlsson. 'Industrial Dynamics.' Technological, Organizational, and Structural Changes in Industries and Firms, Springer Science & Business Media, 12/6/2012

Sarah Monk. 'Job Creation and Job Displacement.' The Impact of Local Enterprise Boards, Department of Land Economy, University of Cambridge, 1/1/1990

Joshua Gans. 'The Economics of Artificial Intelligence.' An Agenda, Ajay Agrawal, University of Chicago Press, 6/7/2019

Maya Bialik. 'AI in Education.' Promises and Implications for Teaching and Learning, Wayne Holmes, Center for Curriculum Redesign, 1/1/2019

Kaveh Memarzadeh. 'AI in Healthcare.' Adam Bohr, Academic Press, 6/21/2020

Frederik Bussler. 'AI-Powered Commerce.' Building the products and services of the future with Commerce.AI, Andy Pandharikar, Packt Publishing Ltd, 1/28/2022

Bernard Marr. 'AI in Practice.' How 50 Successful Companies Used AI and Machine Learning to Solve Problems, John Wiley & Sons, 4/15/2019

Colin P. Williams. 'Explorations in Quantum Computing.' Springer Science & Business Media, 12/7/2010

Marvin Zelkowitz. 'Advances in Computers.' Elsevier, 8/11/2005

Division on Engineering and Physical Sciences. 'The Future of Computing Performance.' Game Over or Next Level?, National Research Council, National Academies Press, 4/21/2011

Jasmine Harper. 'Intelligence Unleashed.' How AI is Shaping Our Future, Amazon Digital Services LLC - Kdp, 4/18/2024

Mansaf Alam. 'AI-Based Data Analytics.' Applications for Business Management, Kiran Chaudhary, CRC Press, 12/29/2023

Joachim Reinhardt. 'Neural Networks.' An Introduction, Berndt Müller, Springer Science & Business Media, 10/2/1995

Yoshua Bengio. 'Deep Learning.' Ian Goodfellow, MIT Press, 11/10/2016

Tom Taulli. 'AI Basics.' A Non-Technical Introduction, Apress, 8/1/2019

Yongbin Ruan. 'B-Model Gromov-Witten Theory.' Emily Clader, Springer, 4/8/2019

Anatoly Liberman. 'Word Origins ... and How We Know Them.' Etymology for Everyone, Oxford University Press, 4/13/2009

John Von Neumann. 'The Computer and the Brain.' Yale University Press, 1/1/2000

OECD. 'AI in Society.' OECD Publishing, 6/11/2019

Computer Science and Telecommunications Board. 'Funding a Revolution.' Government Support for Computing Research, National Research Council, National Academies Press, 2/11/1999

Ray Kurzweil. 'The Singularity Is Near.' When Humans Transcend Biology, Penguin, 9/22/2005